I'm in a giant mansion, wandering from room to room. I open a door and a man runs up to me. "I just have to find someone to celebrate with!" he shrieks. He smiles wide and claps his hands with a bang.

My chest balls into a fist and my breath catches. Where are my children? *Somehow, I know this man is not safe. I start running through the mansion.* I have to find them before he does! *I'm frantically searching, but can't find them anywhere. My heart is pounding and my eyes are wild as I run through room after room, until I finally throw open a door and discover them in bed with him. My heart falls straight down my legs and into the floor as I walk in, laser focused on the scene in front of me, my veins on fire. I can see he's showing them what his genitals look like. I feel I will beat him to death or choke him with my bare hands.*

"Get away from them!" I scream at the top of my lungs, and lunge toward them, waking myself with a jolt, my voice hoarsely crying out in the quiet. The room is stifling hot and I'm dripping with sweat; I realize Josh and I accidentally left the heat on during the night. The sheets and blankets are twisted around me; I feel bound, trapped. I'm deeply disturbed, agitated, and angry—angry about all the children betrayed and abused.

Angry that the case I read yesterday has invaded my psyche. In spite of my efforts to compartmentalize. In spite of the necessity of living a life separate from the monsters I regularly spend time with.

EVIL
AT OUR
TABLE

INSIDE THE MINDS
OF THE MONSTERS
WHO LIVE AMONG US

Samantha Stein, PsyD

CITADEL PRESS
Kensington Publishing Corp.
kensingtonbooks.com

CITADEL BOOKS are published by

Kensington Publishing Corp.
900 Third Ave.
New York, NY 10022

All Kensington titles, imprints, and distributed lines are available at special quantity discounts for bulk purchases for sales promotion, premiums, fund-raising, educational, or institutional use. Special book excerpts or customized printings can also be created to fit specific needs. For details, write or phone the office of the Kensington Special Sales Manager: Attn. Special Sales Department. Kensington Publishing Corp., 900 Third Ave., New York, NY 10022. Phone: 1-800-221-2647.

Library of Congress Card Catalogue Number: 2025935033

ISBN: 978-0-8065-4435-9
First Kensington Hardcover Edition: September 2025

ISBN: 978-0-8065-4437-3 (ebook)

10 9 8 7 6 5 4 3 2 1

Printed in the United States of America

The authorized representative in the EU for product safety and compliance
is eucomply OU, Parnu mnt 139b-14, Apt 123
Tallinn, Berlin 11317, hello@eucompliancepartner.com

Evil is unspectacular and always human,
And shares our bed and eats at our own table.

—W.H. Auden

Author's Note

THE STORIES IN THIS BOOK ARE TRUE. All of the facts of the cases are based on my firsthand knowledge. The dialogue herein is based on my notes, as well as my memory. In spite of my excellent memory, I may not have conversations memorized exactly verbatim. However, what I have written is as accurate and true to the time as possible. I have not exaggerated to heighten drama.

In telling these stories, I have confronted constraints. A psychologist's obligation to keep their clients' information confidential is both ethical and legal. I have therefore changed all of the names and altered many of the details so that no individual could be identified. In addition to using pseudonyms, I have changed ages, birth places, dates, locations, and races. I have not altered the facts of the crimes or my experiences with the clients and in the prisons.

I have made the changes I did for many reasons: to protect psychologist-patient confidentiality; to protect the families of both victims of crimes and of the criminals who commit them (even the families of sex offenders are entitled to privacy and respect); to conceal the identity of those who would not want their association with me revealed, including correctional officers, other psychologists, friends, parole agents, judges, and prosecutors.

Finally I have also changed the names of the members of my family. While my family is an integral part of my story and a source of pride for me, I thought they were all entitled to lead a private and "normal" life, in spite of the intense nature of the work I do and my desire to write about it. I have endeavored to write an honest memoir without revealing confidences, so I have told my story (and the stories of others) in a way that is faithful to the truth as I see it, as well as to the people they feature, without betraying their trust.

Content Advisory

THIS BOOK CONTAINS CONTENT that may be triggering or upsetting to people. There isn't any way to write a book like this without descriptions of abuse and violence, but I have done my utmost to leave out unnecessary details of events and crimes. That said, for some, reading about child abuse, domestic violence, assault, rape, molestation, and other forms of sexual abuse and other traumas may trigger traumatic memories, feelings, thoughts, or associations. If so, I encourage you to seek help and support from a qualified source.

I have written this book, in spite of its challenging material, because it is my utmost hope that ultimately it will encourage a deeper and necessary level of conversation about the issues within.

Contents

Author's Note • vii

Content Advisory • ix

Introduction: Meeting with Monsters • 1

Part One: Committed • 5

    Chapter 1: Heading Out in the Dark • 7

    Chapter 2: Sadist, Psychopath, and Why It Matters • 33

    Chapter 3: Luke • 43

    Chapter 4: Bend 'Em and Send 'Em • 53

Part Two: The Sad Truth • 63

    Chapter 5: Partition • 65

    Chapter 6: "Likely" • 75

    Chapter 7: Tears • 83

    Chapter 8: Dreams and Nightmares • 95

Part Three: Permeable • 103

    Chapter 9: Choices • 105

    Chapter 10: Trial • 109

    Chapter 11: Continuum • 123

    Chapter 12: Tables and Chairs • 131

    Chapter 13: Human • 139

Part Four: Intimately Connected　•　147

　　　　Chapter 14: Achy Breaky Heart　•　149

　　　　Chapter 15: Monsters　•　151

　　　　Chapter 16: Change of Heart　•　167

Part Five: Resolution　•　181

　　　　Chapter 17:　New Pathways　•　183

Sexually Violent Predator Evaluation: Luke Miller　•　193

Welfare And Institutions Code Section 6600 Sexually Violent
　　　Predator Civil Commitment Clinical Evaluation　•　195

Clinical Evaluation: Addendum　•　245

Notice Of Evaluation As a Sexually Violent Predator　•　251

Acknowledgments　•　253

EVIL
AT OUR
TABLE

Introduction

MEETING WITH MONSTERS

’M A FORENSIC PSYCHOLOGIST. This may sound glamorous, but the word *forensic* simply means "the use of science in the investigation and establishment of facts or evidence in a court of law." In other words, my job is to apply psychology to legal situations where it may be used in the courtroom. Sometimes it's exciting; mostly, it's just hard work.

My career in psychology initially began with victims of abuse, and I assumed after receiving my doctorate I would continue that work. However, as I gained more experience, I began to recognize that often the line between "victim" and "perpetrator" was less clear than I'd thought. I worked with a boy who'd been molested as a toddler and later, in elementary school, fondled other boys. I met men and women accused of domestic violence who had powerful trauma histories—growing up in households where violence was commonplace. I learned that trauma work and prevention work were often intimately intertwined: Not every victim becomes a perpetrator, but the vast majority of perpetrators have been victimized.

I began working actively in forensics with sex offenders in 1997 at a clinical training program in San Francisco, a setting where I was in training to become a therapist. It was almost by chance that I ended up at that particular program, and I arrived anxious that I wouldn't be able to feel empathy for offenders. There's constant messaging in our society—through news reporting, TV dramatization, talk shows, etc.—that sex offenders are simply evil and cannot be rehabilitated. But studies and statistics tell a different story, as does my experience working with and evaluating offenders for more than fifteen years. I've been repeatedly surprised by sex offenders' capacity to change when they do the work, and I've been privileged to be a part of the process. I worked in individual and group therapy with sex offenders of different ages, races, religions, genders, ethnicities, and sexual orientations. Throughout that time, I got to know and work with the human beings who committed what our society deems the most heinous of crimes, helping them learn a different way of life—one committed to not harming others.

During those years, in addition to providing treatment, I also gained highly specialized training in sexual offender assessments, honing my ability to assess mental health and deviant sexual diagnoses, as well as for future risk of offense. I worked under the supervision and mentorship of experts, and subsequently I became the one who was presenting at conferences, teaching, and training others.

While my experience as a treatment provider was frequently rewarding, I was well aware that there remained serious sex offenders who fall outside of the norm: those who feel compelled to repeatedly commit sex crimes in spite of imprisonment or intervention. In 2006, I brought my expertise with sex offenders to the California

Department of State Hospitals Sex Offender Commitment Program, where I worked under a law—the Sexually Violent Predator (SVP) Act—that requires assessing sex offenders who had served their prison sentences, but who might still pose a serious threat of committing a sex crime if released into society. If found to meet the criteria of dangerousness of the law, these (almost entirely) men, after completing their prison sentences, go to trial to determine if they should be sent to a locked mental health facility until they're deemed (via new assessment and/or graduation from the program) to no longer be a threat to society.

Evaluating high-risk sex offenders under the SVP law is highly specialized. At the time when I conducted these evaluations, there were almost eighteen thousand licensed psychologists in the state of California and fewer than 110 who performed these evaluations. Expert forensic work as a psychologist in general is rare; expert evaluations and testimony as an SVP evaluator is even rarer. As an SVP evaluator, expertise in the statistics and science of forensic evaluations and knowledge about sex offending are necessary, and having the treatment experience is a bonus—it often helps us form a more nuanced picture of the offender. I never shy away from holding the offenders responsible for their actions and make no excuses for them. But I also have empathy and compassion for many of them as human beings. I've gotten to know so many of them in a deeply personal way, heard their life stories and struggles. So I do not approach my evaluations with damning preconceptions; I individually evaluate each case to determine if the man sitting in front of me is too dangerous, by legal definition, to live in our communities.

This book represents an intersection between my life and the lives of the men I evaluated. As a forensic psychologist, I have had to decide if people who have done terrible things meet the criteria to be locked up indefinitely in a mental institution. As I met with and evaluated these men who committed abhorrent acts, I strived to do my work to the best of my ability and as ethically as I could. I employed my professional knowledge and experience, and met the men with com-passion, empathy, and understanding.

That said, I was and still am more than a forensic psychologist. I also have had a life outside of this work. In addition to interests, hobbies, and passions, I have a family. While I've tried to keep my professional and personal lives separate over the years, it is not possible to separate them completely, and in some ways, I wouldn't want to—my growth and knowledge in one area informs the other. My experiences as a female and parent give me insight in my work, and my knowledge and my experience as a forensic evaluator give me the tools to keep myself and my children safe. As a human being, I have never stopped looking for answers about sexuality, danger, risk, humanity, parenting, and passion—ultimately gaining new perspectives.

It's been several years since I wrote the first draft of this book. In the intervening time, researchers haven't stopped working to make the science of prediction (and, therefore, prevention) better; my evalu-ations might look different, were I to write them today. Also, today my kids are older, our family looks different, and the focus of my work has shifted. Over my more than twenty-five years as a psychol-ogist, my practice has expanded to include many other issues, such as addiction, couples therapy, family work, and people simply want-ing to figure out how to live their best possible lives. But the SVP law has not fundamentally changed, and I believe our need to wrestle with the ethical implications has only grown more urgent. And my work with offenders continues to hold a unique place in my psyche, mind, and heart.

Part One

COMMITTED

The world will not be destroyed by those who do evil,
but by those who watch them without doing anything.

—Albert Einstein

Chapter 1

HEADING OUT IN THE DARK

I WAKE IN THE DARK HOURS of the morning to head out to prison for my scheduled interview with a violent sex offender. By the time I arrive at the prison, our house will be filled with light and commotion, Josh getting our twelve-year-olds, Eva and Rachel, and our nine-year-old, Kye, up and ready for school. But at this moment, the house is dark, still, and quiet. Even Jessie, lying sideways on her ratty dog bed, is motionless. I'll be long gone by the time they all wake.

I meditate, then slip quietly out of the bedroom so as not to disturb Josh. I dress in the bathroom, where I hung my clothes the night before: button-down shirt, blazer, dress pants, glasses, and stylish but comfortable black shoes. My forensic psychologist uniform doubles as an emotional barricade, and as I look in the mirror, I do, in fact, feel armored by its professionalism. I'm not wearing tan, denim blue, or orange by decree—to ensure that in the event of a fight or prison riot I won't be mistaken for one of the inmates and accidentally shot by a correctional officer (CO) attempting to restore order.

Once driving, I'm quickly over the bridge and out of San Francisco; I-80 is deserted in the wee hours. Cool, dark, and lonely is just how I like it. I'm wide awake and ready for whatever's ahead. A day in prison never goes exactly how anyone thinks it will, and the men I meet are always more than their files portray; their files provide the details of their contact with the criminal justice system, but do little to describe the person and his history or what he'll be like to sit in a room with. But I've done this many times before, and the one-and-a-half-hour drive passes without much thought as I drift between stations on the radio.

I arrive at the California State Prison, Solano at 8:00 a.m. The sun is up. I reach the vast parking lot and stop for a moment to take in the trees and fields and to order my thoughts. It's fall, but much of California looks the same year-round, and the area surrounding this prison is serene. There aren't many people who want to live close to prisons, so that's not unusual: a left turn up a bucolic road and suddenly the massive compound appears behind the trees—a large asphalt parking lot and a twelve-foot-high metal fence topped by a roll of barbed wire surrounding a collection of ugly gray concrete buildings.

I park and clip on my prison ID, grab my bag, and walk through the lot to enter the small office at the front of the building, where I show my badge to the correctional officer. He's chatting with another officer and continues the conversation as he checks my ID, gives me a nod, and searches my bag. He hands it back to me after I walk through the metal detector. On the other side, I stand along with the group (attorneys, correctional officers here for a shift change, prison staff) that's accumulated and wait patiently for the door to be buzzed open. We step through and wait for the door to click behind us. After a few beats, a second door clicks open and we enter.

I walk through the prison, a woman alone in a mostly male world. Men in identical prison denim stride through hallways in organized lines monitored by correctional officers in olive drab jumpsuits and black boots. Surfaces are hard and naked, so voices echo loudly and constantly and a kind of noisy controlled chaos reigns. On my first visit to prison, I was shocked to find myself in such close proximity to inmates in hallways and in the yard. I'd imagined the inmates were kept segregated from everyone else. Instead, prison is more like a small town, inhabited mostly by men, all wearing the same clothing with CDCR INMATE lettered across the back. Only, the inhabitants of this town can never leave.

I'm surrounded by the men, the constant sound of voices, of heavy metal doors opening and slamming shut. These days I'm no longer anxious while there, but I'm not completely at ease, either. No one there is.

When I arrive at prison, I've already reviewed most of the records of the men I'm about to meet—criminal records, police reports, court reports, psychological evaluations, prison records, and medical records—but I always read through some additional paperwork that's only available on-site. It's only at the prison where I can find out if he has also committed rules violations while here, and sometimes there is additional information that might be important—notes about jobs he has held and ways he has conducted himself. When I've finished, the officer in charge of coordinating these visits walks me to the interview office and goes to get the inmate. I sit down at the desk, pull out my interview forms and a pen, and wait.

Prisons are very specific about what you can and cannot bring inside—my purse, cell phone, and everything else I've driven with here are locked in the car. I have only my keys, my ID, my inter-view forms, and a couple of pens in my bag. The chair is hard and uncomfortable. It's a medium-sized office, with bare white walls, a desk, two chairs, and a phone (landline). A small window covered with a grate lets in a bit of natural light, but the room is flooded by bright fluorescent bulbs. The place is clean, almost sterile.

I'm prepared and relaxed, mostly at ease, but I have yet to meet this particular man, and his files are replete with violence. I click and unclick the top of my pen. I've read the victims' reports in detail, so I know the violence he's capable of. I've studied what his life as a criminal has been like and how he has behaved in prison. But I also know that a man rarely looks like his prison records. Most often he looks rather ordinary. Dissonance is always a part of this job: the backstory, the violence, and the history versus the person, the human, the face, the eyes, the posture, the thoughts, and the feelings in front of me. I also know, most likely, I'm not the person in this meeting who will feel most nervous today. The stakes are significantly higher for him. For this inmate, my evaluation— my "yes" or "no" decision— could be a part of what determines the rest of his life. This means that every so often my introduction is met with anger. But most of the men are well-behaved and polite, answering my questions to the best of their abilities. They desperately want to go free.

———————

UNDER CALIFORNIA LAW—and in fifteen other states, the federal system, and the District of Columbia—sex offenders who've served time (ranging from a few months to more than twenty years) in prison for serious sex offenses are evaluated prior to their release back to the community. If they're found to lack control over a mental disorder, such that they pose a serious risk of perpetrating future predatory sexual offenses, they can be committed indefinitely to a sex offender treatment program at a state-run mental hospital instead of being released on parole.

My job in this process is to evaluate whether or not these men meet the criteria under this law: I'm required to answer the fundamental question of whether or not this person is likely to continue to commit sex offenses. In real-life terms, it means answering questions such as: Is a man who was hallucinating and strung out on methamphetamines for six days in a row when he raped a young girl still a threat to other children when he's sober and released from serving a twenty-two-year prison sentence for the crime? Should he be locked up indefinitely for a potential future crime he has not yet committed because he *might* commit it?

Because the law is designed to capture only those who show a pattern of sex-offending behavior, of the hundreds of thousands of sex offenders in California, only a very small number end up being evaluated under Welfare and Institutions Code (WIC) 6600—the

Sexually Violent Predator Act. In a year, approximately twenty-five thousand sex offenders scheduled for release from California's prison system are referred to the Sex Offender Commitment Program (at the California Department of State Hospitals) for review. Any inmate who has a conviction for one of the qualifying offenses under the law will be referred; all other sex offenders will simply be released, having served their time. Of those referred, approximately 7,500 are referred for an SVP evaluation; there needs to be at least some indication of a pattern of behavior for an evaluation to take place, since this is the population the law is attempting to capture. Of these 7,500, approximately 1,500 will be found to meet the criteria (described below) of WIC 6600 and therefore face indefinite involuntary institutionalization.

Out of more than 120 evaluations I conducted during the year and a half when this book was written, only 10 percent of those met the criteria for indefinite hospitalization: the average among SVP evaluators. In other words, the men who meet the criteria are not the usual sex offenders who live and work among us, who have made a terrible lapse in judgment, or acted while angry, intoxicated, or depressed, most likely never to do it again. They aren't even the "career criminals" who simply commit an act of sexual violence among a long list of criminal acts over the course of their lifetime. Those found to meet the criteria are the rare men who repeatedly kidnap women and rape them. Or they're sent to prison for molesting a boy, then molest several more boys after being released, then after another imprisonment molest several more boys.

For an inmate to meet the WIC 6600 criterion, the outcome of the forensic psychological evaluation must be the answer "yes" to the following three questions:

1. Has the inmate been convicted of at least one ***sexually violent offense***? Qualified sexually violent offenses are listed in a specified section of the penal

code, and the offender must have used "**force, violence, duress, menace, or fear**" or the victim was **under the age of 14.**

2. Does the inmate have a ***diagnosable mental disorder*** that **predisposes** the person to the commission of criminal and predatory sexual acts?

3. Is the inmate *likely* to engage in sexually violent **predatory** criminal behavior as a result of his/her diagnosed mental disorder without appropriate treatment and custody?

––––––––

THE FIRST QUESTION—has the person committed a sexually violent offense—is fairly straightforward. The law used to read there had to be two convictions under the penal code, but it was changed to one because often people are only charged or arrested for behaviors that never reach the point of conviction. So now they get referred for one conviction and then we see if they've engaged in similar behaviors, even if not convicted for it. The penal codes listed are all sex offenses that include violence and/or are against children. For example, rape and molestation would be on the list, but possession of child pornography and indecent exposure would not. Those offenses are illegal for a reason, and might incur trauma, but this law is designed to capture a very specific type of offender—one who repeatedly commits sexually violent offenses. For this question, the evaluator only has to evaluate if there was "force, violence, duress, menace, or fear," which is a fairly low bar for a sex offense of this nature. If the victim was under fourteen, it doesn't need to be established; it's assumed.

The second question—do they have a diagnosis that predisposes them—attempts to get at the question of compulsion. In other words, does this person have a mental disorder that will compel them to keep committing these types of offenses in the future? For example, if someone was convicted for molesting a child, we would need to answer the question of whether or not they had a diagnosis of pedophilia, because presumably that would mean they have a sexual attraction to children and have acted on that attraction, in spite of the knowledge that it is illegal (and harmful). Not everyone who molests a child has pedophilia, just as not everyone who has pedophilia molests a child.

The third question—are they likely to do it again—will be discussed at length in this book, but in sum we are attempting to use studies and statistics to try to see if someone shares common characteristics with people who commit sex offenses repeatedly. We assess probability. Most people might think this is easy and obvious, but it's far from it. People who commit sex offenses are as unique and diverse as the rest of us. Predicting human behavior is no simple feat.

In order to answer these questions, I must thoroughly review all available records and travel to the prison to meet with the inmate for a two-hour-plus interview. I then must utilize all of this information, along with the current measures, studies, and statistics, to write a thorough psychological evaluation and ultimately answer the above three questions, which typically takes me about thirty or so pages of report to discuss completely.

Some states that have these laws have only one forensic evaluator sent out to evaluate an inmate under the civil commitment law. In California, two evaluators are assigned to independently evaluate the same inmate. If we both come to the same conclusion, which we do most of the time because there is a science to it (imperfect as it may be), the inmate is either discharged on parole (if they don't meet criteria) or is referred to the district attorney for SVP prosecution (if they do). If they do meet the criteria, and the DA takes the case, it goes before a judge for a probable cause hearing; and if the judge sees probable cause, it goes to a civil trial with a jury. The evaluators serve as expert witnesses during the probable cause hearing and the trial. The outcome of this trial is the jury's determination if the individual is sent to the mental health institution indefinitely or released on parole.

If the two evaluators disagree (one finds the inmate meets the criteria and the other says they don't), a third evaluator is asked to conduct an evaluation. It's unusual, but it happens; the science of evaluating human beings is imperfect and has some subjectivity, especially in cases that aren't entirely clear-cut. If the third evaluator finds the person does not meet the criteria for indefinite incarceration, the individual is released. If the third evaluator finds the person does meet the criteria, then the law requires that a fourth evaluation be conducted. So the bar for involuntary institutionalization is high, with many safeguards; in order for a person to be referred for institutionalization under the SVP law in California, they must be found by Department of Mental Health evaluators to meet the criteria of the law by either two out of two, or three out of four, forensic experts. Finally, in order to be hospitalized indefinitely, a judge and jury must agree.

Of the 1,500 offenders in California who are found to meet the criteria for civil commitment under the law each year, only approximately 600 of them may actually be prosecuted in a civil commitment trial and face involuntary hospitalization (the other 900 will be released on parole)—the DA in the county of their conviction makes the call. Of these 600 cases, historically around 450 of them will result in a finding by the jury that the person should be committed indefinitely to the inpatient sex offender treatment program at the locked mental institution.

People often have a knee-jerk reaction when thinking about people who commit sex offenses. It's not uncommon to hear "castrate them" or "lock 'em up and throw away the key." There's a societal, and perhaps even primal, horror and anger about the violation entailed in these offenses. But the truth is, not all sex offenders are monsters or vicious predators driven to abuse women or children again and again. The popular stereotype of the "sick pervert" overlooks the most common perpetrator of sex crimes: your child's uncle, your next-door neighbor whose wife just left him when he lost his job, the kid who was strung out on drugs and made a horrible, life-altering mistake. It's my job to try to help differentiate whether these men, like the man I'm meeting with today, are more unique—a person who is likely to perpetuate these types of offenses again.

AFTER A WEAPONS SEARCH, Joe is led into the room. He's more than six feet, six inches tall; his bulky arms, muscular chest, and broad shoulders are visible under his prison uniform. His bearing is formidable, despite being on crutches due to missing the bottom of his right leg—shot off during a fight in between incarcerations, according to his file. His presence is a visceral reminder of his lengthy history of brutal violence against others, especially women.

In spite of the obvious match between his appearance and the description in his file, I ask to check his prison ID—a license-sized card with his photo and prison ID number. Early on in my work, I started an interview with a man who had the right name, but was the wrong person—the prison had summoned a different inmate with the same name. I can still remember my shock when I discovered the error, thankfully fairly early on—I began to read him the consent form when he interrupted to tell me he hadn't ever committed a sex offense! He was swiftly ushered out and the correct inmate retrieved. This evaluation has severe consequences; I won't be relying on anyone else to make sure I'm with the right person.

Joe's ID checks out. I nod to the correctional officer, who leaves. Joe sits down across the desk from me and I study him as I hand back his ID. Joe is in his late fifties and has an intensity akin to charisma—his pale skin, slow-blinking blue eyes, and incredible calm in the face of what, for most, would be an extremely anxiety-provoking circumstance. I'm aware as I study him that he's studying me in return. I'm not afraid, but I am on alert. This is a typical day at the office for me, but it's never mundane. I'm open and curious, but my boundaries are rock-solid. My senses feel close to the skin and my mind sharp as we assess one another.

The correctional officers down the hall and the personal alarm on the desk are part of the reason I'm not afraid, in spite of the fact that he isn't restrained in any way by chains or cuffs. The alarm looks like a garage door opener. I sit with it directly in front of me. I could grab it if I needed to. I've yet to use one, but I'm glad it's there. Even if I'm taken completely by surprise, correctional officers would be here in minutes to help. Sometimes men know in advance why I've come to see them, but often they don't. I explain to Joe that I'm a psychologist with the Department of Mental Health.

"I'm here to evaluate you," I say to him, "and I'm going to read an explanation of why I'm here. If you have any questions, I will be happy to answer them."

I take a deep breath as I launch into a legally required explanation of the ramifications of the conversation we're about to have, reading the consent form out loud. I say, "You are being evaluated to determine whether you may be a Sexually Violent Predator under Section 6600 of the California Welfare and Institutions Code." I explain the purpose of the evaluation, the process, and what the outcome might mean.

I'm, in effect, telling him this: Instead of being released from prison at your upcoming parole date (for which you've been waiting months, years, decades), you may instead be locked up, indefinitely, in a mental institution. And I'm here to figure out which to recommend. Release or lock up. Joe has just completed serving seven years.

I pause from my reading and look up. The information comes as a shock to most men, so the moment can be unnerving for them, to say the least. For me, it's the moment when the weight of the responsibility and power of my role hits me with full force, every time.

These men know why they're in prison. They know they've been convicted of committing a sex offense. But my words still come as a shock because most of them are not aware of the Sexually Violent Predator Act. Even those who are aware of the law seldom think of themselves as "predators." Most prisoners, like most people, tend to see their lives as a series of random events rather than viewing their actions as part of a malevolent pattern. They are like the rest of us, with problems big and small: the alcoholic who wakes up with a hangover, but thinks, *Well, next time I won't drink so much;* or the mother who feels guilty after smacking her daughter, but thinks, *Next time she'll think twice before mouthing off.* In the back of their minds, they wonder if they might have a problem, but facing that problem is overwhelming, like trying to swim to a shore you cannot see. So, like many of us, they tend to see their lives as a collection of events and choices or decisions that they made at the time and then move on from. They don't tend to look for patterns, or to notice when they occur, and they often don't take full responsibility for many of the choices they make.

I've tried to imagine what it would be like if the tables were turned, if I were the one sitting down with a stranger whose diagnosis could so radically alter the course of my life. How would I process that weight of this moment? How does *he* process it? I look into Joe's eyes and he meets my gaze coolly and simply nods. He has understood and gives off only an eerie calm.

I look down and continue to read, explaining the SVP process. This evaluation doesn't have the usual levels of confidentiality, I tell Joe. Anything he says could go into my report and be heard in court if I testify. I tell him the interview is voluntary, but if he doesn't consent, the evaluation will still be completed, but it will only use legal and prison records.

While they don't want to incriminate themselves by saying the wrong thing (and they are not permitted to have counsel present for this evaluation), most men agree to the interview. They're either afraid to look uncooperative or are looking to tell their own side of the story. Joe simply shrugs, agrees with a nod to sign the consent form. "Let's do it," he says. He signs it and I get out my notepad, ready to record every word he says. Prisons don't allow tape recorders, so my recording is done by hand.

Joe's record reads like the stories that compel lawmakers to be "tough on crime," a criminal record that starts when he's thirteen and only gets worse as time goes on. Between the ages of eighteen and thirty-eight, he was arrested nineteen times: for burglaries, drug possessions and/or sales, selling stolen property, battery, kidnapping, attempted kidnapping, robbery, assault, and various other offenses. Rather than a more typical progression from drugs and burglary to more violent crimes, his records show he was committing whatever crimes suited him, whenever he wanted. Most notable (and the reason I'm here) among the crimes are his multiple sex offenses, which were brutal and intense. He has beaten women and raped them in violent ways. One time he broke a woman's jaw and then forced her to perform oral sex.

I ask Joe to tell me about his criminal history. He replies, "I've got too many arrests to count." And it's true. Even though his last prison sentence was for twenty years, his criminal activity didn't stop once he was on the inside. They never caught him doing anything that warranted new charges, but it's clear he has never been terribly concerned with following rules, regardless of where he has lived. And now he's about to be released from prison, a man in his late 50s, past the middle years of his life—a life spent as a bully, inside and outside of prison.

During the interview, Joe is casual while talking about himself and forceful about portraying his life from *his* perspective: full of contradictions and completely different from the records I just read. Each time I ask him about a discrepancy, he throws back his head and laughs.

"Some people just don't understand me," he says in a slow,

laconic voice. "People exaggerate," or "People just don't understand what's going on." He stares directly at me when he speaks,
a smile playing across his face, his unwavering eye contact daring
me to contradict him.

"It says here in your records that you got kicked out of a therapy group for lying," I say. "Would you tell me about it?"

"Nah, I quit," he replies.

"How do you explain the contradiction? Are the records
wrong?"

"People lie," he says, and shrugs. His eyes meet mine. We
pause a beat.

As the interview proceeds, it becomes clear that he has no
empathy for anyone he has harmed. I ask him about his early
years. He chuckles.

"I remember one time," he says, smiling, "I was little. Maybe
five years old. I used to love to play tricks on my family. One time
I hid out in the backyard after dark. I could see all the lights on in
the house, and I could hear when they started looking for me. They
all freaked—yelling for me, trying to find me. I was laughing when
I finally went inside."

He tells story after story like this, and it becomes clear that
he's very likely psychopathic—someone who truly experiences
no empathy for others—and that even childhood physical abuse,
though likely, can't explain how he turned out this way. My interview includes all of the questions that will allow me to eventually
score him on the Hare Psychopathy Checklist–Revised (PCL-R).
This measure is designed to determine someone's overall level of
psychopathy—a neuropsychiatric disorder marked by deficient
emotional responses, lack of empathy, and poor behavioral controls, commonly resulting in persistent antisocial deviance and
criminal behavior. Once home, I'll calculate Joe's score, but I've
done this enough where I already know how high he'll score.

There's some new research that points to a difference in the
brain structure (in the amygdala) of psychopaths, but it's still

mostly unknown why the rare individual comes along who is unable to feel anything for others. However it happens, this man seems to be one of them. He clinically tells me about severely beating a boy in high school with a rope just because he was "curious what it would be like." He recounts the stories of abuse he has inflicted, as if they were any regular story someone might tell about their life, without feeling or expectations of my reaction one way or another.

One could say I've been presented with a rare opportunity to interview a subject who is a likely psychopath and a potential sexual sadist, and to be honest, I'm fascinated. I tend to think everyone is fascinated by the parts of human nature that are most alien to most of us, but that's probably untrue—not everyone wants to witness and understand the darker, stranger, scarier aspects of being human, like I do. But even with my fascination, the interview takes a toll; as good as I am at staying grounded and compartmentalizing, it's an effort to stay detached. Not because of how alien or frightening the situation is, but because there are ways in which Joe is charming and direct. His lies are clever half-truths, which at times seem almost plausible. I have to continually check my records to stay grounded in the facts.

For example, in the past, Joe told an evaluator he began smoking marijuana daily from age eleven, used heroin for two to three months when he was twenty-six, and called cocaine his "first love," admitting that he used it daily for years. When that evaluator asked him if he was ever addicted, Joe said, "I considered myself addicted to coke at one time, but not anymore . . . I like the high, but not how it keeps me broke. And I don't like the comedown— it's depressing." So when I ask him about his drug use, his answer surprises me.

"It says here you've struggled with a cocaine addiction," I say.

"Nah," he replies. "I was never really addicted to any drugs. I just happened to be around the wrong people and that's the way it is in life."

"But even in your most recent case, you admitted you were using cocaine." I cock my head sideways and use a puzzled tone, confronting the contradiction without confronting him.

He doesn't miss a beat. He leans forward in his chair and props his elbows on his thighs, his biceps flexing. "Some people get off with claims of being high or temporary insanity," he says. "For some reason, that didn't work for me."

As I write all of this down, I become aware that he hasn't actually answered the question, or many of my other questions. His answers lead in circles, or to insinuations, rather than to conclusions. He lies without lying. He talks, but says nothing. Was he lying in the past, or is he lying now? Ultimately, I don't know that it matters as much as the fact that he lies.

There are times when he seems like an ordinary man, and it almost feels like we make some sort of connection. He smiles easily. He's disarmingly warm and charming at times, if prone to the occasional cliché. "People are capable of change," he asserts at one point, "and I have changed for the better."

He tells me his first wife cheated on him. "It was a disaster," he says, shaking his head. "She hurt me pretty bad."

"What about your second wife?"

"Her?" He looks down for a moment, then back up at me. "I gave her everything before she died. We'd still be together today if she hadn't died." He pulls up his sleeve to show me one of his tattoos. "That's her name right there."

"How did she die?"

He adjusts his sleeve as he answers. "She died waiting for a kidney transplant. I offered one of mine, but we weren't a match. She was only fifty-two. I didn't even know how sick she was until she came to visit me in prison and I could see how skinny she was. I didn't want her to visit me because she had to stand in a long line to wait to get in to see me—I didn't want her standing for so long. I quit all drugs for that woman. I'm still not over losing her, you know? It was terrible."

He seems to genuinely care, but it's hard to tell. Even psychopaths can form connections—not the same kind of connection others might feel, but connections, nonetheless. She died after they had been married for fifteen years. I nod—I can't help but feel for him a little. But given his life of violence and disregard toward others, he isn't someone I feel too much empathy for. I let that moment pass. It also doesn't escape me he just contradicted himself, again, regarding his drug use.

Other times his smile is expansive, and he knows the right things to say. I can see how some women might be seduced by him—all of his rape victims were women he knew. When I ask him about his future risk of reoffense, Joe says softly, "It will never happen again. I learned some very important things about myself, and I also try to visualize what the victims went through as a result of my actions."

"What's your plan to prevent offending?"

"To get into some counseling. Some kind of support system. You need a support system. I think every inmate needs that."

If I didn't know him and have all of his records, I might think that was a pretty good answer. His tone is earnest and I'm sure he knows it's the right thing to say. It's work, throughout our meeting, to retain perspective, to figure out who he is and what he's about. I can see how he's good at knocking people off-balance, off-topic, off-center. How it would be moving when he talks about a teacher he admired, or how much he loved his wife. It feels ordinary, until I ask him about charges for almost beating a man to death—or the time his first wife came to visit him in prison, and he lost his temper and began to beat her.

I ask him, as I do all men I evaluate, in detail about each of the sexual offenses he has committed, each of the women who accused him of approaching them seductively before he turned brutal and violent.

"There's a case here in 1994," I say, "when you were reported to have forced this woman to perform oral sex on you, which you alternated with raping her anally until she vomited. Do you remember this case and what happened?"

He laughs. "She was a liar," he says. "She was a prostitute who just wanted to get paid."

My skill at compartmentalization is not just of use when Joe has human emotions, or when he is lying. It's also of use when discussing the horror of his offenses. Every therapist must be able to compartmentalize—to set aside a natural, human, emotional response to pain, suffering, and trauma so that the ability to think and respond appropriately is always accessible. Whether I'm moved or horrified, it can't get in the way of the job I have to do. In the therapy office, that job is to help a client grow from the experience. In an evaluation, I need to remain objective and gather the information I need. For someone who's inexperienced, this might take effort. But for those of us who have a job to do, it's natural. Like a surgeon operating on a child, or a journalist reporting from the scene of a natural disaster—when there's a job to do, emotions are set aside.

Joe laughs off each of the sex offenses, one by one, casually denying any of them happened. It's not unusual for someone to deny committing offenses, laughing or not, so I push him a bit to see what will happen: I let him know that I doubt he's being truthful— that I might not be as snowed as he thinks I am. I'm not expecting much, but offenders with a conscience will sometimes open up when pressed a little. Perhaps I can get him to slip up and admit something.

"Wow," I say, in a puzzled tone, looking up from my paperwork, "what bad luck that all of these women have lied about you. Is none of this true? Maybe *some* of it is true?" I pause and look him calmly in the eyes, waiting.

He sits back and folds his arms, equally calm. "None of it's true," he says, and looks at me with eyebrows slightly raised, daring me to try to get more out of him, confident I'll back down.

His eyes turn cold and without any detectable feeling, and

now my skin prickles. I know that in this moment it wouldn't take much for him to turn violent on me. He is in control, visibly calculating his every word and move. And he doesn't give a damn about consequences. Call button or not, instantly I can feel the vulnerability of my position.

The charged moment passes as I casually move on to the next question, a benign one. I continue to take notes, the evaluation taking shape in the back of my mind. It's my task in this interview to get as much from Joe as possible, both from what he says and from what is left unsaid. I have more than twenty pages of questions to get through, and the rest of our time together moves swiftly. By the end of the two hours, I have a pretty good sense of what Joe is like: a man who does what he wants, looks out for himself, and has little (if any) empathy or care for anyone else.

After my last question, I ask if there's anything he'd like to add or ask, but he just shrugs, half-smiles, and shakes his head. I push back my chair and walk by him to the door to alert the officer in the hall that the interview is finished, careful not to leave my back exposed to him in the process.

I'm relieved the hours-long interview is finally over. My mouth is dry and I'm itching to get away from the prison's antiseptic smell and cold, filtered light. I've been up since before dawn, and the intensely focused state I must inhabit to conduct these interviews has worn me down. I'm relieved I don't have more than one interview today. Sometimes I have two or three; today this one was enough.

The weak winter sun is still high, but has moved to the other side of the sky when I step outside the prison. I shiver a little, but am glad to be out in the air—relieved to be free.

I don't notice the scenery on the drive home. I'm thinking about Joe and the case as a whole: what I said, what he said, what the records said. I'm sifting through it all. There's no question he fits the profile of a psychopathic individual, someone who is completely without empathy. But as far as my job is concerned, that's only part of the question, and not even the most important one. The questions I'll have to wrestle with for my evaluation are: *Why* did he commit the sex offenses specifically, and will he feel a powerful urge to do it again? The law is designed to capture only those who feel compelled to commit sex offenses over and over again because of a mental disorder related to the crimes. I'll have to decide if he fits this profile. It's not a question of whether or not he's a dangerous man. Or a bad man. It's whether or not he's likely to rape a woman again.

I will need to take into account the fact that despite his long, violent history, he has not committed any acts of violence in almost twenty years—either inside or outside of prison—and that he's now in his late fifties. He may not have changed much psychologically, but physically he has, in addition to his missing leg. Even though he's fit and muscular, research indicates that something happens to men as they age—perhaps related to testosterone production—that slows them down and makes them less aggressive or prone to violence.

This case is complex, and I want to get it right. I never see the decision as casual; with someone like Joe, it seems especially weighty. On the way home, I decide I'll consult a colleague or two. In cases where someone is brutal and violent, but may not meet the criteria, it's always good to have a second opinion.

———

THERE WAS SOMETHING HAPHAZARD to the way that I got into this work—the opportunity presented itself, and I found that I was good at it. But what a supervisor said to me years ago still rings true for me and motivates me to continue it: When a sex offender makes changes for the better, it could mean trauma prevention for would-be victims. Offenders work is prevention work; offenders who no longer offend do not create more victims.

The sun is lower by the time I cross the bridge back into the city. I fiddle with the radio and absentmindedly sing along, shifting my mind toward home, my kids, my life. I'm grateful on days like today for the long drive home. It gives me time to leave someone like Joe behind.

I arrive home in time for predinner chaos. Rachel and Eva are in their bedroom at their desks, chatting noisily over pop music as they do homework. Kye stands in the kitchen talking to their dad loudly over the rock music Josh is playing while he cooks.

"Hi, Mommy!" Kye's face lights up when I walk in. They throw their arms around my neck as I bend down to embrace them.

"Hey, sweetie." My shoulders drop an inch, and my heart loosens inside of its bony house as I squeeze them back with a deep inhale, exhale, and a smile. "How was your day?"

"Good." They pull back and return the smile, releasing our hug. "I got an A on my math test!"

"That's great, Kye!" I continue to smile as I straighten and walk over to Josh.

"Hey," I say, hooking my arm around his middle and kissing him hello.

"Hey." He kisses me back. "Dinner's almost ready."

"Excellent," I reply, meaning it. Every part of me is blessing him that I don't have to start cooking right now. "I'm gonna go put my stuff down and change, and then we can meditate?"

"Yup."

"Okay, kids!" I yell. "Almost time to meditate!" I poke my head into the twins' room. "Hey, you two."

"Hi, Mom!" they reply in unison. I'm smiling again.

I walk back down the hall into the small office I share with Josh, drop my bag by my desk, and head for the bedroom. There I peel off my professional armor, down to my underwear, replacing it with my favorite evening wear: flannel pajama bottoms, a tank top, and a sweatshirt. I can feel my body loosen and unwind and I stretch and roll my neck to pull it even looser. The house quiets as Rachel, Eva, Josh, and I sit down to meditate, and Kye begins their walking mantra. The kids were introduced to twice-daily

Transcendental Meditation (TM) when they each were four years old, so they know the drill. It's part of our routine. I had them learn because I wanted to gift them with a practice that could help them through their whole lives, in the same way my parents gifted it to me when I was twelve.

Sitting down to meditate isn't always easy; sometimes it feels like making a dog sit before taking her for a walk. I've been practicing TM for close to thirty years; still, sometimes at the end of the day, I think, *I really don't feel like meditating today,* or *I just don't have time.*

I do it anyway. I have to—it makes me a better person and that makes my life better. When I first started working with sexual and violent offenders, one of my coworkers said he made it a ritual to go home right after work and take a long, hot shower to cleanse himself from the hard things he'd heard that day. I get it. What's a "normal" reaction to interviewing a violent sex offender? My feelings are what anyone else's might be: Sometimes there's empathy, fascination, enjoyment, or fulfillment; often there's horror, anger, and deep sadness.

To be effective at my job, I have to partition these experiences. I have to stay separate from my reactions, thoughts, and feelings about the cases in the same way I do the cases themselves. I observe what I feel and think in the same way that I observe what I hear, see, and understand during my interviews. My focus, effort, and concentration are on paying attention to all cues, both external and internal, and reacting to none of them. It's a deeply felt and rigorous process that goes beyond vague platitudes about maintaining professional boundaries. It also helps me to not react during interviews such as Joe's.

Leaving my interview with Joe today, I walked out to my car and started the process of lifting that partition dividing my inner experience from my observing mind. As the partition lifts, I feel ungrounded for a while. My thoughts swirl as I remember things Joe said, how I felt, moments between us. I think about what's in the files, how he'll score on the risk measures, but I also think about what it means that someone like him exists in the world. What if my children meet someone like him someday? I'm integrating all the information gathered during the interview and forming a picture in my mind, but I'm also integrating the experience into my life, and placing it in my knowledge of the world. In this way, I remain in a healthy relationship with my work—I stay whole with no part of me partitioned off. And it's in accordance with my values in life—I want every experience of my life to be one that I learn and grow from. Become more whole from.

My homecoming is the final stage in my process of reentry. Seeing my family, hugging them, breathing in their smell, taking in their joy at seeing me, their excitement, my overwhelming love for them. I yearn to be fully present with them, to give my family my all. But a part of me is still thinking, integrating, and observing.

So I sit down. The kids go into their rooms to meditate, and I sit down on the big king bed that fills our little room and close my eyes. My mantra comes. Thoughts come; feelings come. The mantra returns. Each time I return to the mantra, my mind gets quieter, more settled. My body relaxes. My mantra comes and I'm transcending until there is nothing. There is only silence. And being. My heart unwraps like a present.

When I open my eyes, my mind is quieter. I have landed, here. Everything in my day—Joe, the prison, his victims, the drive home, my children, Josh, my dog—they're all real, and important. At the same time, they're all ordinary, and part of life. I'm home. I'm fully me, again.

We finish meditating and rise for dinner. Josh and I have been married for our entire adult lives, and we move in a shared rhythm as we go about the evening. Dinner is put on the table, kids are called in to eat, everyone sits and takes a quiet moment to appreciate the meal. Then Rachel launches into a critique of the outfit her math teacher was wearing today.

"Why would she wear that jacket with those pants?" she asks. "They didn't even look good together and were terrible for her body shape. I mean, *really.*" She rolls her eyes. Creating a new look every day is her driving passion; she's acutely aware of the fashion choices of others. Today her hair is fuchsia, her outfit a study in black and white.

"It's true." Eva smiles, validating her twin's perspective. She has a very different look: the neurodivergent, understated, soft, and comfortable tomboy to her sister's curated, girly punk. But she can still appreciate good taste.

Rachel and Eva are fully in middle school this year, and we are all adjusting. Feeling grateful not to be a middle-school teacher, I wonder how long I have before *my* style comes under the microscope.

"There are a lot of complicated factors that go into choosing your outfit," I say, "and not everyone knows how to do it well."

Kye tries to chime in with their own opinions. "Maybe *she* thinks it looks good," they say.

Rachel rolls her eyes. "You're missing the point, Kye. Of course, she thinks it looks good. She has bad taste—that's what I'm trying to say."

"Well, taste is something a lot of people have to learn, Rachel," I step in. I'd rather avoid an argument and there is a middle ground here. "Most people aren't taught what clothing works with other clothing, and they certainly aren't taught what flatters their shape. But also," I continue, "taste is subjective. Different people like different things. What one person thinks doesn't look good, another person might."

"That's fair." Rachel continues eating and Kye nods. She feels validated and Kye appreciates the empathy.

As dinner continues, I feel my heart loosen another notch in my chest, and I'm grateful. Grateful for how these four people root me in the ordinary. There is bickering from time to time, but no one worries about being loved. No one at this table is guarded, including me. I don't have to be careful in choosing my words here or maintain an emotional distance from what's being discussed.

There's nothing magical about this dinner. We pass the salt. We tease and laugh, listen and support, or talk over one another and sometimes lash out in frustration. We connect or fail to connect in all of the everyday ways that families do, and don't. But it is this ordinariness that allows me to breathe and open again. For most of that preciously mundane half hour, I leave the dark, dangerous, and ugly world of prisons and sex offenders behind.

Having unwound from the day, I'm exhausted by the time dinner is over, but cleanup still has to happen. Josh and I chat about our days as we clear and wash dishes, and the kids head to their rooms to finish their homework. I have to remind myself to listen as he tells me about his workday. I'm interested and want to feel connected, despite my fatigue and the distraction of processing the meeting with Joe.

When Josh asks about my day, I carefully consider my response. I feel protective of him and mindful of my urge to unload. A part of me wants to tell everything to him, to process it out loud and get it off my chest. But I'm ever mindful of the psychological effect of these violent, awful cases. It's my job to be exposed to all of this trauma, not his. He has never asked me to shelter him from the details, but I feel instinctively protective of him, and we've agreed this is the best course of action for him. Plus, it forces me to leave my work at work and just be home. I've heard it said that police deal with people at their maddest, saddest, and baddest, and I suppose I've chosen to be involved in something like that, too . . . but Josh has not.

"Well, I had an interview with a 'bad guy' today," I say, a smile at the corners of my mouth.

"No kidding?" he replies with fake surprise, and we laugh.

I reach to hug him amid the running water, wet dishes, and dirty sponge. As he holds me, I feel that maybe, for now, it's enough.

Chapter 2

SADIST, PSYCHOPATH, AND WHY IT MATTERS

L ATER THAT WEEK, I MEET with a small group of colleagues to hash out statistics, risk, and diagnosis. We sit in Martin's psychotherapy office. He's a friend and colleague who mentored me when I started working with sex offenders and evaluating them. The four of us are reclining on Martin's elegant sofas and chairs, alternating between serious, intense, argumentative discussion, and goofing around. We sip our coffee or tea, having carved out a couple of hours in our month to meet in this warm, sunlit room and decipher the dark and dangerous world we work in.

Predicting human behavior is dicey. We can study patterns and become experts in making educated guesses about what might happen, but ours is an inexact science. Still, as a science, it deals in the realm of statistics and probability. Psychologists who research sex offenders design studies that look for the most common factors present when a sex offender reoffends. These factors range from an individual's age (the younger the adult male, the more likely he is to reoffend), to whether or not he victimized any males (more likely to reoffend). Then we shape these factors into tests and measures that we use to place someone in a particular risk category.

If an offender has a significant number of certain high-risk factors, then we say he's similar to sex offenders who reoffend at a higher rate. What comes next? The authors of the research choose numerical cutoffs for categories divided into low, medium, and high, but the law has not tied itself down to these numbers. So it

is up to the individual forensic psychologist (that's me), then ultimately to a jury, to decide whether an offender makes the cutoff for
being legally high risk. Each time new research comes out, we must
fold it into our knowledge base to make our evaluations that much
more accurate. It's a heavy responsibility, but thankfully, we are
only a part of the decision—the experts preparing the evaluations.
Ultimately, the attorneys must make their cases and the judge, and
eventually the jury, must make the final decision. It's just up to us
to do our part the best we can.

At some point in today's meeting, I move the discussion to Joe,
the man I interviewed yesterday. I can discuss the case freely here
because none of these colleagues is the second evaluator on this
case. It's rare that the initial two evaluators will come to different
conclusions—it's happened just once on a case of mine—but it does
happen. If it happens in this case, these colleagues will have to pass
up the case. Having already discussed it with me means they cannot evaluate him fully independently.

"I'm trying to figure out if he's a sexual sadist, a paraphilic rapist, or just a run-of-the-mill psychopath," I say, taking a sip of my
tea, the steam fogging the room in front of my eyes for a moment
before I set the cup down.

"Did he admit to any kind of arousal from the rapes or the
pain he inflicted?" asks Martin, the sturdy, bearded facilitator of
the group, always ready to jump in and help us wrestle with the
issue at hand.

"Right, the obvious question," I reply. A sexual sadist would
get pleasure from inflicting pain during sex, and a paraphilic rapist
would enjoy raping women. "But, of course, this guy didn't admit
to anything. Not a single thing." I sigh and drop my hands to my
lap. "I tried, but couldn't get him to budge."

Steve, the studious, most intellectual member of the group,
jumps in. He has done a fair amount of research on psychopathy.
"Of course not," he says, crossing his left leg over his right, "unless
he's stupid, he's not going to tell you that."

"Hey," says Owen without missing a beat, "I've encountered stupider." Laughter bubbles into the room as we all nod. He's not alone—we've all been surprised by the choices people make during interviews. I once had a man admit to more than thirty rapes he committed during burglaries of women's homes, even acknowledging how much he enjoyed it. He had only been convicted of a few. I was proud to have gotten him to talk about it, but stunned that he would admit to something that would seal his fate.

"Too true." Steve nods.

I have a deep respect for the colleagues who help me challenge my thinking and grapple as deeply as possible with the questions that face me. It's one of the things I love about the work—being forced to constantly challenge my assumptions and way of thinking. I think this is probably something that many, if not most, other evaluators love about it as well, and I cherish the consultation group we've formed that does just that. But we also sometimes need each other for comic relief, lightness, and fun. We couldn't be more serious about the work we do, but to have some relief, we need to laugh together, too. All three of these guys are intimidatingly smart, and very funny—the perfect combination for meeting about these cases.

"Can you see a pattern to his rapes?" asks Martin, getting us back on track. "Usually, the sadists and paraphilic rapists have a certain way they like things."

"That's what I've been looking for," I reply. "But I just don't see it. He's consistently brutal and lacking in empathy, but everything else seems like random opportunity." I flash back to my meeting with him, to what I know about him. The only pattern I can come up with is a consistent lack of empathy and easy power and charm.

"Sounds like a typical psychopath to me," Steve says.

I nod. This is what we have trained and studied for years to do—to look at the chaos and darkness of violence, victims, drugs, criminal history, and individual psyche, and put it all together in a form we can make sense of. In this case, a "typical psychopath."

But every person we evaluate is unique, and each evaluation poses a new challenge. I want to be certain, so I point out that Joe forced his girlfriend to perform oral sex on him after breaking her jaw. It's hard not to imagine the pain, a broken bone, pressured again and again.

"I think that might be sadistic behavior," I say. "There's no question it was painful for her. Was he getting off on it?"

"Maybe," says Martin as he nods thoughtfully. "Or maybe he really just doesn't care. He wants oral sex and doesn't have empathy for her experience at all."

These are the fine distinctions we are required to make—was it sadistic or simply without empathy? Most people might think, *Who cares? It's horrible either way!* And, of course, on a human level, those people are right. The women he has victimized have suffered terrible trauma. And for that, he has been convicted and served a lengthy time in prison. But for my work, these distinctions are crucial. While the idea of setting someone like Joe free is not something I relish, being a part of locking him up after he served that time for something he *might* do is not something I ever take lightly. I have to give each decision I make under this law my fullest consideration. I have yet to perform an evaluation on someone who was found not to meet criteria, then been convicted of another sex offense . . . that I know of. But it could happen. Not meeting the criteria of "likely" doesn't mean *"won't."*

We finish talking about Joe and move on. Each of us takes a turn to discuss a case with our colleagues, challenging each other and helping to think it through. We each bring our own areas of expertise, knowledge, experience, and ways of thinking. With difficult cases these differing perspectives are invaluable. When we are done, we chat a little as we gather our things and then head back out into the sunny day that awaits us. In spite of my gratitude for these gatherings and the insights my colleagues have shared, I often come away from these meetings shaken by our ability to turn the darkest events and philosophical issues into pragmatic, mundane discourse. The question of "risk of reoffense" is at the core of our work. We examine the newest studies as we try to determine how legal terms like "high risk" and "likely to reoffend" translate to the real world—the world in which our evaluations determine whether or not a human being should be locked up indefinitely and we weigh the risk of release against the possibility that another adult or child will be victimized, traumatized.

I get into an elevator with a woman who is holding shopping bags from nearby department stores. I'm certain she isn't thinking about psychopathy. It's jarring to feel the odd juxtaposition of everyday life coming up against my own.

LATER THAT DAY, I call an evaluator in Southern California who has expertise in sexual sadism. I'm getting close to a decision, but Joe has an extreme history of violence, so I want to be as confident as possible in the decision I make. Ultimately, the consultation validates my thinking. Joe has done things that appear sadistic and degrading, but after listening to the case as a whole, the expert is of the opinion that he has not demonstrated the kind of consistent, ritualistic, sadistic behavior of a typical sexual sadist. He might just be an ordinary psychopath; I can't prove otherwise.

Sexual sadists typically have habitual sadistic acts that they perform again and again, and from which they derive pleasure. Without an admission from Joe, or descriptions from the crime reports, there isn't evidence of sadism. There isn't, in fact, evidence that Joe is driven by arousal at all. Clearly, there *is* arousal involved—he was erect, he ejaculated—but the question is arousal to *what*? Something sexual happened, but what *drove* it? What turned him on? Was it his victim's fear, resistance, pain, or terror, or was he immune to their experiences, simply wanting sex and taking it from a woman's body without regard to her wishes?

In Joe's case, there doesn't seem to be a sexual or sadistic pattern, just a pattern of violence that fits with the rest of his life. In other words, there is compelling evidence that Joe has a condition of some sort that has predisposed him to repeatedly rape women; even if he's not a sadist, his lack of empathy has compelled him to repeatedly take what he wants. If he wants something and doesn't want to purchase it, he steals it. If he wants a woman sexually, he takes her. Because he feels little empathy, that feels like the same thing to him.

However, when it comes to the final hurdle of deciding whether or not he meets the criteria as a sexually violent predator, he doesn't make the cut. The reason? I don't have the proof I need to make a case that he has not slowed down—as a typical over-fifty psychopathic rapist would. Most of the time, age slows or stops psychopaths, and the last time this man raped was twenty years ago, in spite of periods of time when he has been on the street. He has been in prison for most of that time, but statistically speaking, because of his age, the risk measures place him in a category of "moderate" risk rather than "high."

In order for an individual to meet the criteria as a sexually violent predator, he must meet *all* of the criteria laid out in the law, not just parts of it: He must have committed a sexually violent offense; he must have a mental condition that would compel him to commit future sex offenses; he must be at high risk to do so. Joe only meets two out of three, so I'll have to make a "negative" decision on this case.

It's the right decision, but I'm not entirely at peace with it. Joe has brutally terrified and either raped or attempted to rape six women. He's the worst kind of criminal: a psychopath with no regard for people or the law. I feel little empathy for him and no desire to free him. Men like him are part of what motivates me to do this work: to make society safer from people who will continue committing crimes. I don't believe treatment would be helpful for him. Treatment for psychopaths is controversial at best; there is no evidence it works, and some fear it can make them more effective at being manipulative. But to release him back to the streets is unnerving.

A few days after turning in my report, I find out that the other evaluator on the case came to the same conclusion. Joe will be released from prison a free man.

I resign myself to the fact that in this case, as in all cases, I can't do this work unless I can set aside my feelings and do the best possible job. The law has been written to ensure that only people with the highest risk of harming others can be indefinitely committed to a hospital for a crime they have yet to commit in the future. They must meet all of the criteria under the law, or they must be released. To take away someone's freedom indefinitely after they have already served their sentence for a crime is not something to do lightly. And Joe does *not* meet all of the criteria the law outlined, which means that society must figure out some other way to deal with him. What that should look like, I don't know. I'm neither lawmaker nor judge nor jury. I don't have a magical intuition. I have a job, and that job is to apply forensic psychology to the law and vice versa, and to see if it fits a particular person. In some ways, I'm simply a witness, laying out the evidence as clearly as possible. If I'm to continue to do this work well, my role has to remain, as the 12 steps would put it, "right-sized." I cannot minimize it, but I cannot overstate its importance, either. I just need to apply the law, as written, to psychology, the best I can.

Still, my role in Joe's release from prison is one of those moments that makes me shut my eyes, take a deep breath, and say a prayer: "God, please don't let me have been wrong." Judaism has taught me it's part of my purpose on earth to make the world a better place—"*tikkun olam*" means to "repair the world"—but sometimes how to go about doing that doesn't feel so simple. I know I can't predict the future, and unless for some reason there's press, I'll likely never know what happens to him. He could be an outlier, someone who doesn't fit the statistical probabilities. In real-life terms, that means he might victimize someone else—and my "negative" evaluation would have played a part in giving him that opportunity. Moderate risk doesn't mean no risk at all. Thankfully,

I'm aware that ultimately it isn't my job to ensure everyone's safety in the world, nor can any of us live a life without risks. I can only do my job—predicting future risk—as accurately as possible, to the best of my ability.

———————

THE SEX OFFENDER COMMITMENT LAWS, like the SVP law we have in California, are, by their very nature, controversial. No other convicted criminals—not arsonists, robbers, kidnappers, assaulters, drug dealers, gang members, repeat drunk drivers, repeat domestic violence perpetrators, stalkers, white-collar criminals, or even murderers—are evaluated, postsentence completion, in this way. As a culture, we have singled out sexual and predatory crimes as so heinous and dangerous that we are willing to preemptively keep these citizens confined. Not unlike the way we have detained "enemy combatants," when faced with fear of future risk and in the absence of other options, we as a society choose to have sexually violent offenders detained. Having served out their sentences— some of which are quite lengthy—these inmates believe they have earned the right to parole like any other criminal who has "served his time." They were sentenced and have been punished. My job is to walk in at that moment, sit down, face them, and tell them that they may, instead of going free, be committed indefinitely to an inpatient sex offender treatment program in a state mental hospital. And then I ask them to tell me their life stories.

Finding out about this evaluation, and the potential repercussions of it, is a shock to most of these inmates, and often their reaction can range from fear to anger to outrage. The California SVP law was enacted in 1996; the first such law was enacted in Washington State in 1990, following several high-profile rapes and murders. However, few people know about these laws—and sex offenders are no exception.

My responsibility as an evaluator is tremendously weighty. I'm faced with the choice of recommending that someone be locked up indefinitely or be released and potentially harm more people. It's also complex ethically, because the right answers are apparent only in hindsight; tasked with the job of predicting the most likely future, society will only know if we have gotten it right when the future arrives.

The civil commitment process is fraught with challenges. It is extremely adversarial. There is deep passion on the sides of both those who support and oppose this law—some feel it a necessary evil, others feel it infringes on our fundamental rights as citizens, a law designed to punish a politically unpopular class of individuals. In practice, it exposes the real limits of science and research. The science of prediction is good—it's based on research. But it's also imperfect—human beings, by our very nature, are unpredictable. Also imperfect is our legal system, which disproportionately sentences people of color and those with less financial means. And while a person's race, ethnicity, sexual orientation, and financial status are not statistically correlated in any way with risk of reoffenses—and therefore not specifically relevant in the work that I do—it is, horrifyingly, a factor in whether or not someone is arrested and/or incarcerated, to begin with, and is therefore a factor in whether or not they end up sitting across from me for an evaluation.

For all of these reasons, the SVP Act is highly controversial. But in spite of that controversy, few people are questioning it in a real, deeply personal, and thorough way; the discussions are limited to psychologists, researchers, and legal scholars through articles published in trade journals. As I do this work, I can't help but think we all should be wrestling with it. If we as a society continue to single out this set of crimes as deserving indefinite confinement, we should at least discuss, argue, and wrestle with the implications. After all, these are human beings, fellow citizens with complex lives and histories. They have committed unspeakable acts and yet most of them feel they have changed, believe they would never commit such an act again, and they have families who love them and want them to be free. Some of them deny having even committed those acts, and they may not have. While there are people who would deny the humanity of these criminals because of what they've done, the fact remains that they are, in fact, fellow human beings. Keeping society safer is about keeping real people safer, but locking people up without just cause creates a world for all of us that is not just. All of these questions eventually come to the fore for me in the case of Luke Miller.

Chapter 3

LUKE

Several weeks after meeting Joe, I'm at Mule Creek State Prison seated across from a man who is friendly, but guarded, and has several visible prison tattoos. Luke Miller is in his mid-thirties, with dark hair, is of average height and weight, and seems always in motion—picking at his clothes, fiddling with the edge of the table, and constantly shifting in his chair. I introduce myself, he signs the consent form, and we begin the interview.

Luke is probably as relaxed with me as he ever is, which is to say *not very.* He bounces his right leg throughout our time together, frequently leaning back in his chair, at times tilting it back to balance on the back two legs. He makes little eye contact with me—looks everywhere else in the room as he answers my questions. As the interview progresses, I'm aware his answers are rife with contradictions from previous reports I've read, and often I'm confused about why he would be lying about some of the things he lies about. It makes sense he might lie about his criminal offenses, but I'm puzzled why, for example, he tells me there are no mental disorders in his family. Previous reports say both of his parents were on medication and he has a brother who's mentally ill.

We begin his interview by talking about his childhood. I learn Luke's behavior problems started when he was young; he tells me he was frequently sent to the principal's office, got into fights with other kids in the neighborhood, and was expelled from sixth grade for fighting. I ask him if, in addition to fighting, he was lying and stealing.

He leans back in his chair and crosses his arms across his chest. "Yup. I stole a lot. I used to break into houses—steal from people and sell their stuff to get money." He shrugs, then adds defiantly, "I'm sorry, but I did."

Many of his answers during the interview are accompanied by a shrug. He shows little emotion throughout our time together, and the shrug seems to be his way of brushing off any concern others might have about his behavior. "It's no big deal" seems to be his consistent attitude, regardless of the topic. I make a mental note of his shrugs, of the times he says, "I'm sorry, but . . . "—by which he means he's *not at all* sorry. In many ways, Luke seems just like so many offenders I've met with—full of bravado, calloused, used to a life of crime. I remind myself to keep an open mind with him, to see him as a unique individual who might surprise me.

We move on to talking about Luke's substance abuse. He tells me it began when he was twelve and continued into his adulthood—he went from sniffing paint with friends to methamphetamines by the time he was fifteen. He used meth daily until his most recent incarceration. I ask him if he thinks of himself as addicted and he doesn't hesitate to answer.

"I'm addicted, yeah. It's a big problem in my life. I know I'll have to do something, or I'll end up in jail the rest of my life." He pauses briefly, leaning his chair back to balance on the rear legs. "Sometimes I take more than I mean to, and it makes me think things that aren't true."

I pause, wondering if there is an opening here to some emotion. "Like what?"

"Like I see men on the street as ready to steal my car and take my money. One time I was so overamped, my friend had to hold me back from leaving the house." He shakes his head and laughs.

I pause, letting that hang in the air between us. Letting the laugh pass into quiet. His answers make me sad; I wonder if he has insight about it. "Have you ever tried to stop?"

"Yeah, but I always go back. Most I've been able to stop is a couple months." His characteristic shrug makes an appearance, brushing off the possibility of feelings, in spite of the struggle that's implied.

I press on. "Hmm. Any other drug use? Alcohol?"

"No. Every now and then I drink to come down from the meth, but that's it." The front legs of his chair land with a thud and he leans forward across the desk to punctuate the definitiveness of his answer. It's clear he doesn't want to be challenged.

I lean back slightly in my chair. I'm not afraid, just sending a signal to respect my space. My movement causes him to settle down and lean back, but it's clear he's a man who has little understanding of or control over his emotions, not just by the way he acts during the interview, but because his life and criminal record are peppered with impulsive acts, addictions, and eruptions of violence. I later discover what he has said about other drug use is another lie: Reports state that he's used marijuana, acid, and PCP, and has abused alcohol regularly—on one occasion was drunk when arrested after a high-speed chase by police.

Throughout the interview, I sit with Luke the way I sit in every assessment—relaxed and neutral, so he feels confident and comfortable. This is not anything I was taught or trained to do, just a style I've developed over time with experience. I've become an expert in reading facial expression and body language out of necessity, and thus have become equally expert at using my own body language to communicate. I sit facing Luke, nod as he speaks, and clarify in an encouraging way. I keep my facial expressions neutral and my face and body open. This encourages him in the same way it encourages all of them; they aren't being judged, and they know it. This gives me the best shot at getting him to open up and show me who he is. It works pretty well—sometimes too well if I let it carry over to my life outside work. I have to be extra careful at parties; otherwise, people end up saying things about themselves that are probably better left unsaid—things that are deeply personal that they might feel overexposed about later. Of course, that isn't my concern in these interviews. I move on and ask him about his relationships.

"Do you have friends?"

"I have a few friends." Luke shrugs again. "They all use meth with me. I don't like using it alone—only with people."

A rare acknowledgment that other people matter. That relationships matter. I note this, warming to him a bit. "What about romantic relationships?"

Another shrug. "Nah. I've only had onetime things."

"Onetime things?"

"Yeah, you know, just like a one-night stand with other dope users, here and there. I want to try to have a relationship, though. I don't know how to have a responsible relationship with a woman."

Another flicker of insight and longing. It's not much, but it's something—he has the desire to form attachments. He's not so cut off that he's lost the yearning to form connections. But when I ask him about any significant romantic relationships at all, Luke tells me he has a daughter, eighteen years old, who lives with her mother in another state. He's had no contact with either of them since his daughter was born and hasn't provided any support. He says his wages will be garnished when he's employed.

"I see. Have you ever been employed?"

"Not really." He shrugs again. "Well, I had a job for a year and a half when I was sixteen. I bagged groceries. And I've worked when I've been locked up. But nothing else on the outside." The truth is, he has barely spent time "on the outside," so it makes sense he hasn't seen his daughter or provided for her. He continues to show little emotion about it all. It makes it hard for me to feel much for him, in spite of how sad his life has been.

I ask him more about his one-night stands. "How many do you think you've had?"

He shrugs again. "Maybe one hundred times total." He pauses, then says defensively, "But some have been with the same woman, more than once."

I plow forward. "Have you ever hired a prostitute?"

"Yeah."

"How often?"

"Eh . . ." He shrugs. "Just once or twice."

I'm skeptical if that's true. If he's having sex with other addicts, it's likely he's trading drugs for sex. I let it slide—the answer doesn't make that much difference. But it does make me wonder about his level of manipulativeness.

"Have you ever told a woman you loved her just so she'd have sex with you?" I keep my tone neutral.

"Yeah, I've done that." He's either honest because he doesn't think any of it is a big deal or because he's unashamed. I can't tell. Either way, it doesn't look good.

We move on to discussing Luke's criminal record. This is the center point of an interview, where I can get a lot more information than may be available in the charges and convictions on his rap sheets, or even the police reports. It's here I look for patterns of behavior, see if I can get them to acknowledge things like arousal or preplanning. I also look for things that might mitigate risk, such as insight, accountability, and relapse prevention planning.

Luke's contact with the law started when he was young and never let up. His first police contact was at fourteen years old when he was picked up for skipping school; his official criminal record begins at the age of fifteen, and by the time he's seventeen, he's had eight arrests and five convictions. He has barely spent any time outside of jail or prison since then.

When he was seventeen, Luke was convicted for assault with intent to commit rape. He broke into a woman's home, removed her baby from her sleeping arms, and attempted to rape her, threatening to kill her. Her fighting and screaming caused him to flee the scene. This offense seems to show little empathy for her terror or her fear of harm to her baby. I ask him to tell me about how it went down.

"Well, I broke in cuz I wanted to steal her VCR. Then I saw her sleeping there. I took her into the bedroom and cussed her out. She started screaming and I just left." He shrugs again, showing little feeling about what he's done or the impact it may have had. I'm unimpressed with his accountability, empathy, or insight about it.

Luke's criminal activity continued after his release from that offense. At twenty, he was arrested in a stolen vehicle with a thirteen-year-old, where they had parked to "get romantic." After that, he had a myriad of arrests and convictions, including rules violations in prison, through to the age of twenty-five, when he again broke into a home and attempted to rape a woman who was sleeping.

"What about this arrest?" I ask him neutrally, looking through my papers. "Back when you were twenty-five and you broke into that woman's home who was sleeping?"

"It sort of happened the same way." He shrugs his customary shrug. "I thought no one was home, saw her on the bed, roughed her up, got scared, and left."

He undoubtedly wants to quickly move past these questions. I work to slow him down. It's clear he's brushed over much in his life. My job today is to try to do the opposite. I need to evaluate, as much as I can, what motivates this man.

I pause and knit my brows. Maybe if I can gently push him a little further, he'll admit to his intent. I keep my tone soft. "Were you trying to rape her?"

"I don't know." Shrugs.

"Hmm." I pause, not wanting him to feel defensive, but sensing an opening. "What do you think? You did get convicted of attempted rape."

He rolls his eyes and rubs his palms on his thighs. "Yeah, I guess I was trying to rape her."

He shrugs again, then folds his arms across his chest, daring me to ask him more questions, but that's not necessary. I exhale. He has now admitted to two attempted rapes, even though he was only charged with one. That's significant. The offense he's currently serving time for—and about to be released from—is for a third attempt to break in. High on methamphetamines, he attempted to open the window of a home where a woman was sleeping with her five-year-old disabled daughter. When he couldn't get the window open, he went around to try the door, then tried to force the door open with his body weight while she called the police.

I ask him about this offense, too. It seems so similar to the others, but he denies a connection. He insists this wasn't another attempted rape—he was just running away from someone and decided to hide in this woman's house. I find it difficult to imagine he's telling the truth.

In spite of his lying about some things, Luke has surprised me with how forthcoming he's been about the attempted rapes. It makes me wonder if he'd admit to a desire to rape and a plan to do it.

"What about these attempted rapes, Luke? Was it really just a fluke, or did you break into houses hoping you'd find women there to rape?" I spell it out for him so he can answer as simply as possible if the answer is "yes."

"Nah, I didn't plan it or anything. I was planning to rob the houses and just found them there. It was a spur-of-the-moment thing."

This is often how break-in serial rapists who are aroused to rape start: They break into a home and find a woman there and rape her. Then they do it again. Eventually they begin to seek out the experience. I decide to push him—he has actually admitted to rape fantasies in the past, and this would be key information for my decision.

"Okay. But, Luke, in your records from when you were locked up at the prison hospital for a while, it says you've talked about having fantasies about raping women. About cutting them and raping them." I confront him but my tone stays friendly. Warm. As if I'm just trying to understand.

"Yeah, well, I said those things, but I was lying. I just wanted to stay in the mental health ward and not go back to prison."

He is referring to his time in the prison hospital, which are the records I'm referring to. His records from that hospital stay say that he told the staff he regularly fantasizes about cutting and raping women, including a nurse at the facility while he was there. They also don't believe he was faking anything; he was given multiple diagnoses—from personality disorders and substance use disorders to mood and delusional disorders—and put on medication. In his discharge report, they stated that he was a "danger to society . . . a threat to public safety, especially to females he comes into contact with." Luke admits to none of this to me. Of course, who could blame him?

It's time for me to wrap up the interview. I end the interviews by asking what would prevent offenders from committing another sex offense? "Three times you've broken into women's homes and attacked two of them, and you haven't ever been out of prison that long," I say. "What's your plan here? How are you going to make sure it doesn't happen again?"

He pauses to consider, looking down, then looks up with another shrug. "Drugs. I need to get my endorphins some other way," he replies.

I wait, but he says nothing more. That's the extent of his "plan." In other words, he doesn't have a plan to prevent another crime from happening or understand how to control himself. Sobriety would be a good start for him, but it would just be a start, and that isn't something he can see today.

On my drive home, I mull over my time with Luke. I tried to like him, but he didn't offer much that's likable. He seems to show little regard for others' experiences and has little insight about his criminal history and harm to others; he pays lip service to having some remorse, but whatever he feels hasn't stopped him each time he's been released. He isn't the worst I've encountered—he was more honest than many and he seemed to have potential on a human level—but he mostly seemed to care for himself. I'll need to run the statistics on this case and weigh it out carefully, as I always do, but it's not hard to guess how my decision on this case might go.

Chapter 4

BEND 'EM AND SEND 'EM

A WEEK LATER, I'M OUT TO INTERVIEW another inmate and I leave the house feeling light and at ease, camera in hand to take photographs along the way there and back. The photos I'm taking these days are not just photos for photos' sake. Each time I head out for an evaluation, I'm attempting to capture my experience in a way that words can't express. In the absence of being able to photograph the inmates I evaluate or the prisons (illegal and a violation of confidentiality), or myself and my family (unsafe), I'm photographing the roads and vistas between these places, trying to match the outer journey with the inner one.

This creative act changes the whole tenor of the experience for me—it makes it feel almost as if I'm traveling for my art, and the interview in the prison is something I'm doing on the side. My career as a psychologist is one I enjoy, and it's how I make a living and support my family, but any day that I can make art is a good day for me, so bringing my camera along for the ride makes my chest feel immeasurably lighter. I feel compelled to take these photographs and can feel aliveness behind my eyes when I think about what they might be able to portray. How they might show what I don't have words for. As a result, I don't feel nearly as heartbroken about what I hear and see as I might otherwise, and the long delays at the prison don't get me down. The day is for my art, as much as anything.

As I take these photos today, my biggest concern is that they won't accurately portray the heaviness of the experience—the weight, sadness, loneliness, emptiness, dissociation, dislocation, and absence of humanity—in spite of the fact that it's winter and everything looks muted and cooler. It makes me so happy to take them, and I worry my joy and excitement will leak into the photos and take away from their pensive nature. But then, maybe that's okay. It's me taking the photos, just as it's me interviewing the inmates. Maybe what's important is that I'm taking photographs, and that somehow, through all of this, I've retained some of my creativity, optimism, and joy. That's worth a lot.

I arrive at the prison and soon I'm interviewing James, a man who has a laundry list of crimes starting from when he was a middle schooler—a long rap sheet that encompasses pimping, stealing, and assaulting others, including several sexual assaults. He also committed a sex offense in prison: indecent exposure to a prison nurse.

During the interview, I can see he's a "smooth operator"; it's obvious he's experienced in talking his way out of trouble much of the time. He speaks slowly, his eyes lidded, and pulls out clichés by the fistful. "You know?" he asks at the end of every sentence, habitually seducing agreement out of whoever is listening. He gazes at me as he answers my questions, a smile playing on his face. He makes everything an inside joke and laughs easily, but almost nothing he says is funny to me.

Throughout the interview, I remain neutral. I want him to talk as openly as possible, so I aim to make him comfortable. I appear open enough to form a connection, then knock him off balance every now and then with a question he doesn't expect, but one that hits the mark. This way he knows that I'm too smart to be suckered like most people and he has to be honest, at least some of the time. I allow him to talk about school with bravado, then suddenly empathize with how hard it is to struggle with subjects you don't get.

"It's hard for kids who struggle," I say. "A lot of times, they get into trouble because they're embarrassed."

He pauses, the smile still on his face frozen. He looks down. "Yeah," he says. "I didn't love it."

He quickly goes back to his bravado, but moments like these

remain in the room, like ghosts of a different conversation, keeping things more honest. It's a cat-and-mouse game, although obviously it's not recreation; the consequences could not be more serious. I ask him about high school. He says he was pimping by the time he was sixteen; his cousin initiated him into the business.

"Yeah, I was good," he brags. "I would bend 'em and send 'em."

I take "bend 'em and send 'em" to mean that he had sex with the women who "worked for him" whenever he wanted. I refrain from making a face. I ask him, just to be sure, "What exactly does that mean?"

"I was born hung." His chin lifts, again the smile playing at the corner of his mouth. "I can stick my magic wand in them and show them the ropes before I send them out there to do their thing."

"So you were 'training' them."

"Got that right." His smile widens. I repress the urge to reach over the table and choke him. There is something about his smug view that women's bodies are his to use for his pleasure and profit, and his unabashed admission—even pride—about it, that makes me angry.

He goes on like this during the interview, talking with relish about his penis size, his sexual prowess, the ways he's used women. As he talks, my stomach is tight and I can taste metal in my mouth. The sexism and misogyny are so extreme, it almost seems unreal. I write it all down, thinking about how he's so caught up in the pleasure of himself that he forgets whom he's speaking to, and the consequences. Or maybe he doesn't have any awareness of how he sounds. Speaking to me, he uses my first name.

"I was always a ladies' man, Samantha." He smiles broadly.

"Dr. Stein." My face flat, I meet his gaze. "What, exactly, do you mean by that?"

"Well, I don't know how to say it better than that, Samantha. I just seem to have my way with the ladies. They can't get enough of me. I can't tell you why." He leans back in his chair, still smiling.

"Dr. Stein." My voice and face still flat, weariness of this game barely disguised, I write, word for word, what he has just said, and review my notes to move on to the next question. Before I can ask it, James abruptly inquires if I've published an article in a pornographic magazine about how to stimulate women.

"You look familiar," he says. I look up from my writing and see his shirt elevated by something from below. "That article was really helpful," he continues. "I'm the king at eating women out, making them relaxed to receive me. You look just like the lady that wrote that article. I loved that article." He keeps talking, looking at me, touching his shirt. It takes me a minute to realize: *Yes, that really is his erect penis under his shirt. He's touching himself.*

I look directly into his eyes. "Are you stimulating yourself," I ask without asking, my voice expressionless and my face tight. "You need to stop immediately."

"Nah, nah, I wasn't doing nothing," he replies, quickly adjusting his pants, sitting up in his chair.

I take a deep breath and compose myself. My stomach is tight, and I can't quite feel my feet on the floor, but I want to complete this interview. I'll deal with my feelings later. I could justifiably end the interview now, but I want to get as much information from him as possible, even if I'm doubtful I'll need it for a decision.

Honestly, I'm stunned. Not so much that he would do such a thing, but by his lack of control. He's sitting in a prison with someone who holds the power to recommend he be committed indefinitely based on his sexual behavior and he sexually acts out. That said, my words have had an effect. For the rest of the interview, he refers to me as "Doc" and does not touch himself again.

After the interview, I report his behavior to the prison; he'll get written up for it at minimum. My final evaluation states that he meets the criteria as a sexually violent predator; his actions during the interview were just one more example of how little restraint he has when it comes to his sexual behavior. It takes a lot to shock or even surprise me these days, but I'm a little floored when I think about him after I finish the evaluation—his lack of control, his disregard for women, the audacity to think he can get away with anything;

his egoism that I would believe his bullshit stories, his arrogance that I would sit there while he got himself off.

————

IT'S BEEN SEVERAL WEEKS and it's time for me to make the decision on Luke Miller's case. SVP evaluations are always completed on a deadline—we are sent out just prior to their release, and must make a decision before their release date. If this were Canada, they would have been evaluated before sentencing and gone straight to the treatment program rather than serving a long sentence in prison first. But here, they serve their time in prison, and then, if they qualify, in a hospital prison after. Luke's release date is rapidly approaching. A decision needs to be made.

I think through my decision about Luke's case carefully as I type up his report and calculate his risk levels. Technically, Luke is a "wobbler"—not completely cut-and-dry. He only has a single qualifying offense. If this evaluation was simply based on his criminal record, I'm not sure I could find that he meets criteria. Additionally, while one of the risk measures puts him in a "high-risk" category, the other puts him only at "moderate high."

But that isn't the only information I've got. Part of my interview is aimed at gathering enough information for me to be able to score the Hare Psychopathy Checklist–Revised (PCL-R). I score Luke and his score places him at the 76th percentile compared to other male inmates, meaning he has a lot of the traits associated with psychopathy. Luke has lived a life of crime without much regard for impact on others. He lies, he manipulates, and he's impulsive. He admits that he lies to women in order to get them to have sex with him.

Furthermore, after I complete the evaluation, more information comes in, including a penile plethysmography (PPG), or phallometric assessment, done on him while he was in the hospital. The PPG measures blood flow to the penis while being exposed to different stimuli. While it cannot be used to predict future risk of reoffense, it does indicate what someone is aroused by. Luke's PPG indicated a "deviant sexual arousal pattern with a preference for aggressive sexual acts directed against an adult female"—in other words, rape turns him on. During our interview, Luke admitted to attempting to rape at least one other woman than the conviction he has on record. Also, he acknowledged to his treatment providers that he was regularly getting women so drunk they were not able to protest having sex with him. All of this, and he seems to lack real insight about his issues, and he's a chronic methamphetamine addict with no history of sobriety and little impulse control.

I complete my report and turn it in: *It's my opinion that Mr. Miller does meet the criteria as a sexually violent predator as described in Section 9900(a) of the Welfare and Institution Code.*

———————

THAT EVENING I HEAD OUT for a walk after the kids are in bed. I'm stressed—about money, about getting work done, about not having exercised. With three children and a mortgage, there's never enough time or money. I'm the biggest wage earner right now, and it feels like I'm always trying to outrun the tidal wave of enough—working enough, making enough. If I had more financial freedom, how might that affect my choices about work? I might continue to do the work I'm doing, but I might not do as much of it.

I walk fast to try to get my heart rate up, to get the workout I desperately need. As I do, I'm alert to the places the moonlight and streetlamps don't reach—fresh after completing Luke's evaluation, I'm a little vigilant. A lit cigarette in a doorway—is the person male or female standing there? I wish it didn't matter.

I used to walk back to my car at night through a rough neighborhood after running treatment groups for sex offenders. At the time, my work actually made me less afraid—knowing that stranger assaults are less likely, feeling a (false?) sense of security that I would not be attacked by a man who knew I had the phone number of his parole officer. And I enjoyed running the groups. I genuinely liked many of the guys and knew they respected me, even felt protective of me. I felt, and still feel, at home around men, having worked with them for so many years.

But on a larger scale, after reading about hundreds upon hundreds of victimizations, sexual abuse by men feels inevitable and unstoppable. Preventing it, at times, feels like trying to head off a wildfire by spitting on it—that men, as a whole, pose a terrible threat. Josh, male colleagues, my friends—they all live on the same continuum with "bend 'em and send 'em" James, break-and-enter Luke, and psychopathic Joe.

For the past several years, I've been providing clinical supervision for a woman who's been treating sex offenders while accruing hours toward her licensure. She's in her early thirties, living with her fiancé, and is disarmingly open about her thoughts and feelings, including her thoughts about intimacy. It's a pleasure for me to offer the space for her to grow and learn about how to do this challenging work. The space between us is warm and honest.

Recently, after some time speaking about her patients, there was a pause and she abruptly asked, "Does this work ever affect your opinion of men?" She went on to talk about a recent group she led.

"The men all talked about how at some point in their life they'd had affairs and lied to their partners. I kinda got freaked out and went home and asked my boyfriend if he ever cheated on me. He was like, 'What? What are you talking about?' After I explained what had happened, he was understanding about it, but the whole thing made me worried about how I was thinking about men—like they're all kinda out of control sexually."

Quiet, I took in what she'd said, reflecting on my own experience. For a moment, I considered offering her reassurances, but decided to be honest. "Unfortunately, this is not an idle worry." My tone is soft as I speak slowly. "Is it possible to see hundreds of men who've harmed people through their sexual choices and not be changed?"

"Yeah," she said softly. "I guess that's true."

"Maybe the task isn't to not be changed; that's just not possible. Maybe, instead, it's to not become jaded. To work to love individual men. And to be able to hold on to compassion for the mistakes of being human."

"Yeah," she said, "that makes sense. That's a goal I can work on."

The truth is, even good men in my life, whom I love and trust, have made mistakes along the way, acted unconsciously sexually, and have broken trust. I wanted to offer her something certain to hold on to, but I know that all people who work with the darker parts of humanity have to figure out a way to still feel love and hope.

All I can think of is to share what has worked for me, and remind her that most sex offenders are men, but most men are not sex offenders.

I want to be able to help my children with this, too, but I'm not sure how to do that while educating them on safety. I use my knowledge of criminality, statistics, and risk to give them practical advice. "Tell me if anyone does something that makes you uncomfortable, or touches you in places that are confusing," I tell them. "Even if it's someone you know and like, or trust." It's practical—if they're molested, it will most likely be by someone they know—but it's painful. I've also used my knowledge to help them safely get help, if they need it. I've never told them: "Don't talk to strangers." What if they're lost and they need help? Instead, I've told them: "If you get lost, look for a mommy first; if no mommy is around, look for a woman."

My children are safer that way, statistically speaking. But, of course, there is a deeper, implied message: Men are more likely to be scary and dangerous. Even if you know them. I worry what that message will mean to them. Will it make it harder for them to trust men? To see them as safe? Ultimately, I worry what that message means to me, too. I never want to lose sight of their individuality. Of their humanity.

Part Two

THE SAD TRUTH

The sad truth is that most evil is done by people who never make up their minds to be good or evil.

—Hannah Arendt

Chapter 5

PARTITION

A COUPLE MONTHS LATER, on my way out to another prison, I take a wrong turn and find myself lost. I'm grateful, for the hundredth time, for the GPS on my phone. Most prisons are located out in the middle of nowhere—among farms, grazing cows, or out in the desert—so there are often no street signs and no one around to ask if you get lost. I used to frantically call Josh on the phone when that happened, asking him to figure out where I was on a map on his computer and direct me . . . that is, if I could even tell him where I was. We were both relieved when GPS became available on phones and I could get myself to the prison without his help.

It's my guess prisons are built way out there because most people don't want to live next door to a prison. It's not particularly unsafe—escape is pretty rare—but I suspect it's that people don't want to look out their window every day at the giant, fenced-in complex next door. It's an eyesore, not to mention one that's a reminder of how vulnerable we are. I get it.

In the end, my GPS comes through and I arrive, only to end up waiting around for the interview in the common area. Several prisoners and a couple of COs inquire what I'm doing here, initiating the conversation by asking me, "Are you a psych?" or just assuming and calling me "Doc" the way everyone who works in prisons speaks to psychologists. I begin to wonder if I have the word "psychologist" tattooed across my forehead. Is there something about me that broadcasts it?

The CO who is my liaison eventually comes to get me and informs me I will have to conduct my interview today in a "phone booth"—slang for talking through glass on phones. This is the least desirable way to conduct an evaluation—to ask someone the intimate details of their life over the phone and through glass—but I comply, trusting the judgment of this CO, who believes this inmate might be dangerous and is concerned for my safety. The man has become angry and threatening lately after discovering he won't be released as scheduled and is being held pending my evaluation. It's unlikely I'll be harmed, but if the CO feels there's a chance, it's not one worth taking. He's apologetic, but I thank him for his concern.

I suppose in some ways this is what this work is about: trying to assess risk and create safety. To place barriers between those who cause harm and their potential victims. To try to assess dangerousness, the best we can, and act accordingly.

The interview itself is uneventful. He's respectful and answers all of my questions. I'm fairly confident before the end that he'll be released.

———————

MY FORENSIC JOB IS ABOUT ASSESSING where a barrier should be placed to keep offenders away from victims. As a parent, my job is to try to place the barrier on the other side—in front of my child. Over the weekend, I check my email when I get home from buying groceries and see that I have one from Rachel. I didn't have an email from her before I left, so I look at the time it was sent and see she sent it while I was out. My heart sinks as I realize she has gone on the internet while no adult was home; this is still strictly prohibited in our house.

I know this rule won't last, just as I know we'll be buying a cell phone for her and her sister soon, in spite of my original idea that we'd wait until high school. The tidal wave of electronic media will soon crash over our home, just as it has over everyone else's, and I simply will have to do my best to set whatever limits I can. I also know that I don't want to create an atmosphere where lying and sneaking are the norm. I have two preteens now and, in the blink of an eye, I'll have three teens at home making a lot of decisions on their own. My job is to prepare them for this the best I can, not make rules that they figure out how to work around behind my back.

All of that said, Rachel did break a rule and I caught her at it, and it's dangerous for her to be on the internet unmonitored. So I call her into my home office to speak with her about it.

I take a slow, deep breath. I long for this to be a normal parenting moment about limits and common sense rather than about the sex offenses that threaten to invade the safe island I call home. And yet it informs me and my choices. How could it not?

I meet the gaze of this kid I love. "Rachel, I know you went online when I wasn't home today."

"What?" She looks startled, quickly debating whether or not to deny it.

"Look," I say, reaching out and taking her hand, "if you don't like the rules, tell me about it. I would rather compromise than have you lie and sneak. Would you do that, please?"

Rachel looks down and away. "Okay," she replies, sighing. "Sorry."

"You know I have this rule for a reason, right? For your safety." My mind flashes to the millions of graphic, extreme, disturbing porn out there on the web, flickering just out of sight, a click or two away from my daughter's fingertips. "I know I've told you there is a lot of graphic stuff on the internet that would be unhealthy for you. Harm you. Just as there are people on the internet that could harm you." I pause, reaching for words a middle schooler would hear. "I want you to have the freedom to do what you need and want. I just want you to have it in a safe way."

"Yeah, I know." She rolls her eyes and takes her hand away, but then looks down again. "I just needed to check my email. I haven't had a chance to check it all week!"

I believe her—at twelve and still fairly innocent, she's not going to get into too much trouble yet. But I know this won't be all she's doing for long.

"I know, sweetie. I get it. I really do. Just wait until I get back and you can check it then. If you feel like for some reason you can't wait, then at least check in with me about it."

"Okay." She sighs again, then turns and walks out of the office, heading back toward her room.

We'll see how it goes. The conversation felt like a decent parenting moment, but it didn't address the fear at the pit of my belly about my children's access to the internet. I can try to protect them, and prepare them, but ultimately it isn't in my control.

—————

ABOUT A MONTH AGO, a twenty-five-year-old kid walked into my office at work asking if I could help him with an "addiction" to child pornography. I have continued to see patients for therapy while I conduct evaluations. Not many—just a couple of afternoons a week. It feels important for my mental health. Evaluations are rigorous and interesting and pay well, but the clinical work is about helping people grow and change—make something different with their lives. It's more hopeful, positive work.

This young man shared his struggle with me with his mouth turned down throughout the session as he struggled not to cry. He told me that he'd discovered rape pornography on the internet when he was eleven years old and masturbated to it throughout his teens. Then, while file sharing one day, he accidentally downloaded child pornography. He knew it was wrong and felt tremendous shame, but he also felt a rush of excitement at the forbidden. Now he couldn't stop himself from going back to it, again and again. He was able to stay away for a few weeks at a time, but has ended up back there again, masturbating.

Regular kid, good upbringing, loving family, no desire to molest kids.

"I'm not religious in any way, but if this were a couple of centuries ago, I feel like I would be going to a priest to try to get this demon out of me." His voice trembles and he looks down, then up again to meet my gaze with a plea.

"Well, thankfully, we don't need a priest for this work. We just need you to be committed to the process and some insight, practice, and time." I smile warmly.

"I'll do everything you say." He smiles in return, the first time since he came in, his eyebrows parting a little on his forehead. "I'm all in. I just want to stop." He pauses. "I mean, I want to have never started, but I can't undo the past. So now I just want to get where it can all be part of the past."

I've come to believe there's something about unfolding sexuality that is tender, precious, and imprinting. Some of what we desire seems to be innate, but some of it's about discovery of what feels good, what is exciting, what is arousing. So similar to baby birds or animals that imprint on the animal that cares for them—whether a dog or a pig or a human—and then follows that animal around as though it were their mother. We seem to be imprinted in our tender years by whatever we discover that is exciting, erotic, or pleasurable. That then becomes the pathway we travel, again and again, reinforcing itself with the pleasure it produces each time. Discovering sexual pleasure is a way of learning about yourself in a whole new way—different from any other learning that comes before it. There is so much possibility for beauty . . . and equal possibility for pain.

This young man and I work together for a couple of years, helping him to abstain from the dopamine pull while simultaneously retraining his sexuality into something more intimate and healthy and getting his excitement elsewhere. By the end of the treatment, he's free from the compulsion and dating a woman he loves. It feels like a win for us both, but it's painful to know how preventable his suffering was.

In the kitchen the next morning, I watch Eva and Rachel chat and maneuver around each other and me as they make themselves lunch for school. They're tall, slender, and beautiful in completely different ways—one a strong swimmer, with long, dark, wavy hair and olive skin; the other a fair, willowy dancer, with brown curls. They look confident and happy and they're mostly innocent to the world of sex. Yes, they have had a thorough education about sex and relationships, but it is just beginning to shift and sprout internally for them, like the seed that swells before the first shoot emerges. Tiny beginnings of adulthood sprouting.

The protectiveness I feel about this part of their life is fierce. Of course, I want to protect them from all sorts of things I can't: the meanness of other kids, the experience of feeling left out, the stress about grades, even the confusion about sex and partnering. Clearly, that's not possible. But premature exposure to the intense, graphic, and often deviant world of sexuality on the internet—or, God forbid, actually meeting someone like "bend 'em and send 'em" James or being asleep peacefully at home when someone like Luke breaks in—strikes a different kind of fear in me. It could turn them off from the joy, intimacy, and specialness of sex, or it could traumatize them or eroticize a world that will lead them into profound suffering. Either way, it would rip them from their own experience of discovery. The profound hope that I hold for them is that their process of exploration and unearthing is positive and loving, with the partner of their choosing.

As soon as they go off to school, I'm on the internet figuring out which blocking and tracking software I will buy. I can't monitor them all the time, and it feels like they're wandering into dangerous years. It makes me uncomfortable; it feels controlling, untrusting, and intrusive. I don't purchase it today. But I know I eventually will. There is no way to keep my children completely safe from someone like James, Joe, or Luke—or anyone, really. But damn if I won't do all I can to try.

———————

A COUPLE MONTHS LATER, I'm writing an evaluation on a man who molested a six-year-old boy—the son of his girlfriend. They were living together and the man did things with the boy as if he were a full, adult sexual partner. I'm recording the account of the boy, verbatim, for my report, when I start thinking about what I'm writing.

My youngest, Kye, was assigned male at birth and is only a few years older than this boy. I remember what six looks like; I was just there. I shut my eyes as I'm flooded with tremendous sadness for this little boy—his innocence and openhearted state, just learning about the world and how to give and receive love. I imagine him earnestly trying to follow directions, to please this man who takes care of him, even as he may feel shame, confusion, fear, or even revulsion inside. My heart hurts in my chest.

———————

RECENTLY AT A PARTY, I got asked, yet again, how on earth I ended up doing this work. I told the woman the truth: I started working with sex offenders by accident. In 1997, I was in a doctoral clinical training program, and I got placed at an internship site that worked with domestic violence perpetrators and sex offenders.

"Did you have reservations about working with them?" she asked, no doubt putting herself in my shoes.

"Let's just say that I'm not different from anyone else." I smiled.

Of course, I absolutely had fears about doing the work, and I expressed them to my supervisor when I first started my internship.

"What if I have no empathy for the people who do these terrible things?" I asked. "Is it possible to have empathy for people who seem to feel little of it?" I also worried I'd be overwhelmed by my feelings for their victims as we talk about what they've done. "What if I can't mask my anger or fear or disgust? I'm supposed to be their therapist."

I expressed fears about my capacity to do the work, but I had fears for myself, too. *How would the work affect me? What will it turn me into?*

My supervisor was kind in his response, but honest. "You are not alone in having these questions"—his eyes met mine with seriousness—"and some of them will only be answered by giving it a try. But regardless of whether or not you decide to do this work, you will not remain unchanged by the experience." I could feel my heart beating in my chest as he paused, then continued. "No one is. It will affect every part of you—your thinking, your emotions, your sexuality, your relationships, and your dreams."

My stomach clenched at the prospect, but I appreciated his frankness. Knowing the truth landed me back in my seat. My head swirled at what it all meant and what it might be like, but the prospect of something that could change me so powerfully drew me to it like a magnet. I just had one more question.

"Are you glad to be doing this work?"

"I love it." He smiled warmly. I couldn't help but smile in return.

To my surprise, I found that I loved it, too. Up until that point, I had been working with survivors of trauma, which was profoundly rewarding, but heartbreaking. Years later, I spoke with a forensic psychologist at a conference who told me that, like me, many sex offender treatment providers began with victim work. "Then we get tired of pulling bodies out of the water," she said, "so we decide to go upstream and try to prevent them from going in, in the first place."

I'll never forget my first appointment with a sex offender; I was asked to observe an intake—a client's first session with the clinic where information is gathered about their history. I could feel my heart beating right out of my chest. As the intake therapist asked details about the man's life and his offenses, my head swirled with thoughts. The frankness of the conversation with the perpetrator was something I had never witnessed—this was before crime shows proliferated on TV or documentaries interviewed perpetrators in front of the camera. I had never heard about sex offending from the offender's point of view.

When asked about his sex-offending behavior, the man spoke about having molested children—several boys he encountered in public bathrooms. As he spoke, my jaw tensed. I felt protective of the boys and outraged at his crimes. I wanted him punished. I wanted him stopped.

Yet, during the rest of the interview, the man seemed completely ordinary. He had an average build, was kind-looking, and was more nervous than I was. He spoke softly and looked down with intense shame as he talked about what he had done. With the exception of his offending behavior, there was nothing exceptional about him, and I found myself feeling empathy for him as he spoke about his difficult childhood, his work life, his family, and his dreams. In spite of his abhorrent behavior, he was strikingly human.

By the end of the session, I didn't know what to think or feel. But I knew I was changing already.

———

TODAY I'M IN MY HOME OFFICE, trying to finish the evaluation on the man who molested the six-year-old boy, when Kye comes in.

"Please, Mommy," they say plaintively. "Can I go shoot hoops at the playground by myself? I'm bored. The playground is half a block away! I could just bring my basketball. I'll come back whenever you want." This is something they've been asking for weeks.

I look up at them, my young, sweet, happy child beaming at me with their most darling, winningest smile. There's no need for them to convince me—I know they're capable. But they want to *prove* to me they're capable, too, grown-up enough to walk to the park and back alone.

"What about Eva and Rachel? Can't they go with you?" I ask

lamely, wishing they'd want to go with them, but already knowing the answer.

"They don't want to go." They fiddle with my pen on the desk.

I glance over at Josh, also in the office working, as a last-ditch hope, even though I know he's too busy to go shoot hoops. Josh hasn't even paused or looked up from his work; it's likely he hasn't heard any of our conversation. Usually, these types of decisions are up to me anyway. I look back at my kid, still fidgeting with items on my desk, waiting patiently.

Everyone can go to hell, I think. *My children have to grow up with confidence. And stranger assaults are rare anyway.* Knowing the facts helps me overcome the often-irrational, media-induced societal fears.

"Okay," I say finally, the word coming out slowly. "But set your watch alarm for thirty minutes, and come back as soon as the alarm goes off, okay?"

"Yay! Okay!" they shout over their shoulder, running off to get their basketball and slamming the front door behind them.

I'm happy and excited for them.

And then spend the next thirty minutes trying not to look at the clock, the hands of which seem to move very slowly.

Finally Kye bursts through the front door, completely delighted and proud, and runs up the stairs to where I sit.

"Here I am, Mommy! Back at two, just like you said!" They're breathless, cheeks rosy from the cool outside air. I, too, am proud—of them and of myself. We exchange high fives, and they run off. I turn away, relieved—not realizing I was holding my breath, until I exhale. Even if the scientist in me knows harm to him was unlikely, the parent in me couldn't help how I felt anyway.

Chapter 6

"LIKELY"

WHEN I LEARNED THAT the United States Army uses the term "servicing the target" to talk about shooting any target, including human beings, I was shocked. It's quite the euphemism for killing someone. But, in truth, the language of my work isn't so different. My colleagues and I discuss a sex offender's "risk of reoffense," because that's the central legal question. We look at the newest studies and ask questions about how to most accurately determine "high risk" and "likely to reoffend." These terms hide the real questions and dangers behind them. What we really mean is, are they likely to rape or molest someone?

Like the U.S. Army, we use terms that are practical, but amoral, and stripped of emotion. It's an easy way to help us distance ourselves from the powerfully evocative work that we're doing—to help us think about it all in unemotional terms. We are all human. Compassion for other human beings—in this case for victims—runs through all of us whether we like it or not. Language can create intimacy and connection, but it can also help us create a barrier necessary for the task at hand—for those of us who need to not think about the potential victims too much.

Predicting human behavior is impossible. It's like predicting the weather—we study patterns and become experts in making educated guesses. And they're both governed by the same ultimate truth: While we can get pretty good at it, there is no way to predict the future with 100 percent accuracy. That doesn't stop us from trying; we research, we design studies, we look for patterns of reoffense. We study what's true about the lives and crimes of those who do it again. We shape these factors into tests and measures that we use to compare. When we complete these tests and measures, we can say: This person is similar to a group of people who reoffend at a higher rate than others.

The central legal question of our evaluations is whether a person is *likely* to commit another sex offense, due to their mental condition. As a forensic evaluator, I must look even more closely at these terms than the people who wrote the law. What exactly is a higher rate? What *numerical value* constitutes "likely"? Researchers have chosen cutoffs for low, medium, and high based on generally accepted ideas about those categories, but it's researchers who have done this, not lawyers. When this law was passed, it was challenged in the courts over the question of what "likely" means, and the legal decision was very specifically nonspecific; "likely" was not given any numbers or percentages. It doesn't even mean "more likely than not." It just means "likely."

This means it is up to the evaluators, the courts, and the jury to decide if an individual is legally high risk and likely to reoffend. How do we make that call? Very, very thoughtfully and to the best of our ability. New research comes, reevaluations are made, new assessments are carried out. We constantly hope for more accuracy. This is especially tricky in cases like Luke, where the numbers don't neatly add up.

Like all ethical forensic evaluators, I'm up-to-date on the latest research, so my reports are good, and as accurate as the current knowledge base will allow. But, of course, I can't predict what some future knowledge may bring to the table. Will a new discovery change the answers? I attend presentations, meet in small discussion groups, and wrestle with new information—new terms, studies, and statistics. The questions seem ordinary and factual, but they're less than ordinary, and none of it is mere fact.

Today at my home office, I'm wrestling with a decision on a report that seems borderline. The man has qualifying sex offenses and a mental disorder that would compel him to commit the crimes. So my decision comes down to evaluating his level of risk. I look at the studies: A score of 5 corresponds to a recidivism rate (rate of reoffense) of 25 percent within ten years—meaning his score makes him similar to 25 percent of sex offenders who commit another sex offense within a ten-year period.

For some, 25 percent might feel like a comfortable cutoff; a common risk-level cutoff score for forensic psychologists is 33 percent and this is generally comfortable for me. My colleague Steve justifies it by saying, "If you had a thirty-three percent chance of crashing every time you took a flight, would you fly?" Most people wouldn't.

But close to that borderline, the ground feels less steady. What if the risk measures puts someone at 31 percent risk? Or even 32.5 percent? Does that mean he's no longer likely to reoffend? Martin, my friend and colleague in this work, sends me a quote about how when you're the type of person to live your life in color, it's hard to describe the truth in black and white. This resonates deeply with me, but it doesn't resolve my decision on the case I struggle with today.

In desperation I turn to Josh, asking for advice from someone uninvolved, whom I trust. Because we are officemates when I work at home, because he's smart and insightful, and because we are close, Josh ends up participating in my work from time to time, in seriousness and in the way he makes me laugh.

Like most people, I need to talk about my work sometimes, and he's been interested. Sometimes I just talk with him about it in the mundane way anyone might talk to their partner about their day at work; other times I might run some aspect of a case by him (without violating confidentiality, of course). I've tried to be thoughtful about what I expose him to and to not talk about the work all the time or fill in the details too much so as not to subject him to the trauma of it. But that's not always easy to do. As a result, he's come to learn about the world of prisons, violence, sexual offenses, criminals, impulses, and psychology, whether he thought he wanted to or not.

In this case, I'm wrestling with logic of sorts and he seems like the right person to run it by. He's an engineer by training and computer programmer by trade. "Measure twice, cut once" is one of his favorite aphorisms. He listens to my dilemma over numbers and responds calmly, referencing baseball.

"I think the tie goes to the runner."

I feel momentarily relieved, and then confused. "But who the hell is the runner?"

"Well, that's the question, isn't it?" He smiles. "Do you err on the side of protecting society or protecting civil liberties?"

"Great, thanks for the help," I say, and we laugh. I would love for him to make this decision for me, but it's mine to make.

I return to my task, and the unanswered question awaits me: *Does it seem like this guy will probably do it again?* Never far from my mind when I grapple with this question are all the possible outcomes. The two that haunt me the most are these: *If I say yes, and I'm wrong, he may be locked up indefinitely for a not-good-enough reason. If I say no, and I'm wrong, another human being could be terrorized, molested, raped.*

After setting aside my own thoughts, feelings, and judgments, I complete the required tests and measures one last time. I consider all of the many variables and answer the legal questions and finally land on a decision that seems the most accurate to me: He does not, after all, meet the criteria. I feel the decision is the right one, but I never forget what these decisions imply.

To complete my job, I was required to make my decision and weigh in. But I'm grateful I don't have the final word; I couldn't do this work if this ultimate decision were up to me. The second evaluator, the judge, and the jury will all contribute to the final call. One person alone could not possibly bear the burden of a decision like this, especially when the real-life ramifications are too big to imagine.

———————

THE OTHER DAY, I WALKED into my twins' bedroom. "Hey," I inter-rupt their chatting and giggling. "I was thinking maybe you guys wanted to go on some outings on your own these days. On the bus. You two have done some short rides. I think you're ready to go places. And you could eventually take Kye when you get comfort-able with it."

While many parents these days are anxious to encourage their kids' independence, I know what I was capable of at their age and what they are. I want to encourage self-confidence. I want them to believe in themselves that they are capable of navigating the world.

"By ourselves?" Eva's surprised, but pleased.

"Yeah." I sound more confident than I feel. "Why not? You guys are ready. That way you won't have to always depend on Dad and me to take you places. Why don't you take a practice ride together?"

"That'd be cool." Rachel responds with a casual demeanor, barely covering her excitement.

"That *would* be cool!" Eva's not hiding her enthusiasm. I can see they're proud, and I'm proud of them.

But when the day of their practice outing arrives, my pride gives way to nervousness and the certainty I had felt about their readiness evaporates. *What have I done? Am I crazy?*

"Okay, you guys have your bus money?"

"Yes, Mommy," they reply in unison. Rachel rolls her eyes, while Eva holds up the money. They look at each other and giggle.

"All right, all right. Just checking." I know it's not necessary. They're both competent, responsible, and ready. It just gives me something to focus on.

I walk them down the stairs and out the front door. "Have fun, you guys." I give them each a kiss.

"We will!" A chorus, again, followed by laughter. Having twins has been fun.

I watch them walk, arm in arm, down our block toward the bus stop with excitement, looking way too young and small for the vast world. I want to yell, "Come back! You're too vulnerable out there alone!"

Instead, I bite my tongue and go back inside the house. I busy myself with work and housekeeping and purposefully avoid looking at the clock. I reassure myself that parents always feel their kids are too young for whatever the next stage is, and the urge to control and protect makes sense but isn't, ultimately, what creates a confident child. They're ready for this and I know it, and the likelihood of them encountering danger is low. A few hours later, they return safely, and more confident and mature. After that, the bus begins to be a regular option for them.

And then there is my youngest, Kye. Some of their friends have been given independence already. This was a freedom afforded to me and my brother at the same age. When I think of my youngest objectively—and lovingly—I see no reason why they shouldn't be able to take their basketball and walk one block to the playground to shoot some baskets by themselves, just like they did the other day. Our neighborhood is pretty safe—one of the safest in the city—and violent crime in general in the United States has been declining for decades, in spite of the constant stream of bad news that would have us believe otherwise (and many parents make decisions in response to). Not only that, stranger assaults are relatively rare. Statistics tell me they're unlikely to be harmed.

But I also know from my work that when there is a stranger molestation, my youngest would fit the perfect victim profile. Girls are most often victimized by family members and friends; fathers, uncles, coaches, dates, boyfriends—these are the most common perpetrators against the young female. But not boys. Certainly, they, too, are sometimes victimized by men they know. However, statistically, if a man is going to molest a stranger kid, it will likely be a child who is biologically male, and additionally a child of the age of my youngest. Furthermore, Kye is beautiful, athletic, confident, social, outgoing, and completely appealing to most people.

I try to be reasonable and encourage independence, but find it hard to stand separate from what I know. I hope I'm not instilling needless fear or sending mixed messages: "I believe you can handle yourself, and I want you to be independent, but I'm scared." Although I don't want Kye changing at the pool in the men's room alone, I have let them go into public bathrooms by themselves. The other day, it took them a while and I couldn't stop myself from embarrassing them by yelling, "Kye, are you still in there?" ("Yes!" they yelled back, and I immediately felt chagrined.)

My colleague Martin tells me that regardless of references or experience, he would never hire a male babysitter. I think about Luke, who keeps getting high and harming people. I think about my kids and the independence and confidence I want for them. I want what I know to help me make the best decisions for them, not take away their freedom. I know I'll never find the right balance. I keep reaching for "likely."

Chapter 7

TEARS

Today I set out to drive for most of the day to the Shasta County Jail. I'm on my way to interview Luke Miller again. It turns out when I evaluated him eight months ago, the other evaluator disagreed with my decision. I'll never know why—we have to write our evaluations independently, so I haven't seen the other. My guess is it's because Luke only had a single qualifying offense. Perhaps Luke didn't admit to the other evaluator his intent to rape in the other case, in the way he did with me.

Because the other evaluator found him to not meet criteria, he was evaluated by two more psychologists, and because they were also a split decision, he was released from prison. It's rare to get two split decisions on a case, but the law is set up for these contingencies. Now here we are, eight months later, because he failed to register as a sex offender—a requirement of him and most sex offenders every year on their birthdays. Failure to register is an automatic parole violation, so he was sent back to jail. Going to jail with sex offenses on his record automatically flags him again as a potential SVP, so now he's being evaluated once more. I was available to evaluate him, so it was assigned to me. By law, the new evaluations will stand as the new decision.

In spite of the nearly four-hour distance, I don't mind the drive to Shasta County. Once I'm alone on the road, I'm alone in my mind. I listen to books and music, sometimes just float through my thoughts. I have my camera with me. Much of the drive brings a sweet smile to my face—the landscape is lovely. I pass trees, cows, grassland,

and farms, small towns and cities. But I'm not after the lovely with my camera. I'm trying to visually capture an experience of this dark world that words can't quite describe. Today may not be a day to take photographs. I listen to NPR until I'm out of range and then hover between stations, trying to find something besides Christian preaching and bad music. I'm expecting my decision will be reaffirmed, in spite of the decisions being so split last time. Luke was full of nervous habits and lied his way through the interview. He was suspicious, a drug addict, and a career criminal, including several attempted rapes. I don't know for sure if he continued to use drugs in prison, but it wouldn't have surprised me.

I arrive at the jail and wait for an hour in the waiting room, which is cold and dirty and smells like sweat and old food. There are signs on the walls that seem to shout out the rules of visiting. Large, bold letters tell visitors what they can bring in, and what they can't; how long they can visit, and how they will be charged with a crime if any rules are broken. I sit on one of the hard plastic chairs and watch family members, parents, friends, girlfriends, boyfriends, husbands, partners, and wives. They have come to visit inmates; some are dragging along young kids, who are bored and whiny. Some visitors try to be discreet and seem embarrassed; they speak softly through the glass window to the indifferent staff, who speak loudly and firmly. It's all business to them and there are no allowances for privacy or for shame.

After my hour-long wait, I'm finally allowed in to meet with Luke. We arrange ourselves in yet another bare, concrete room. The table is wobbly, and we sit on either side in orange plastic chairs. After greeting him, I ask if he knows why I'm here, and he nods and replies, "To maybe lock me up." I wince internally at that characterization. I want to tell him that *his* choices and actions are what may lock him up, not me. But I also know that ultimately it's my evaluation, along with another, that will trigger the law to keep him behind bars. So I can see his perspective.

As soon as the interview starts, it's clear I'm sitting with a different person than the last time we met. This time, in front of me, I see a man who seems to lay his soul bare. Luke has tear tattoos, two of them, just below the lower corner of each eye. I watch the real tears that run alongside them for the entire hour we speak.

"I'm sorry I'm crying so much," he says, wiping his face with his sleeve. "My therapist says I'm crying all the time because I'm off drugs for the first time in my life. I'm feeling my feelings now."

"Your therapist?" I ask, almost disbelieving that this is the same man I met before. The man I met a year earlier would never have gone to a therapist; nor would he have talked about feelings or have cried openly.

"Yeah," he replies shyly, looking down. "I've got a therapist. He's really helping me."

This time Luke shares more about his childhood—a childhood similar to those of so many men in prison who are also addicts: physical abuse and substance abuse were rampant. He tells me his father died four months ago from cirrhosis of the liver—in prison, where he's been since Luke was in his late teens, incarcerated for a third-strike drug offense. Previously I had asked Luke about his parents' relationship while he was growing up. He told me he has a couple of other siblings and a half sibling, and that things weren't easy, but he had "moved on." He shrugged, telling me his parents had divorced because they hadn't gotten along so well, but his mother hadn't had any serious relationships after that. In this interview, I learn that most of his family was rife with substance abuse and domestic violence.

"My parents used to party a lot."

"*Party?*" I am aware of the term, but not sure exactly what it means to him.

"Yeah . . . you know, drinking, drugs. It was their lifestyle." He opens his palms wide, as if to acquiesce to their choices.

"I see. So the quality of their relationship wasn't so great, probably." I'm imagining the chaos, the effect on the child witnessing this.

He pauses for a moment, then looks down. "No. My dad used to beat up my mom from time to time."

Domestic violence. Again, not surprising with the prison population, but it still makes me sad.

"How might others have described you as a child, Luke?" I like this question; it often gives me a window into the person behind the bravado. Or not. In the first interview when I asked it, Luke was full-on boasting, speaking about himself as a troublemaker. This time the answer touches me.

"I was a playful kid, I guess. Kinda shy. As the oldest, I used to take care of the others—when we were hungry and my parents were too busy getting drunk, I took them to my grandparents' house to feed them. I think most people would've said I was pretty quiet."

I let this sit for a moment, while I write it down, getting a feel for who he was.

I continue. "How were you disciplined as a child?" I ask the question this way because if I ask, "Were you abused as a child?" many, if not most, would answer "no." This is partly because they haven't yet understood it to have been abuse, but also, perhaps, because they aren't ready to think about their childhood that way and how it might have affected them. I ask it again this time, thinking he might have gained more insight.

He looks down at his hands. "We used to get beat up—hit with a belt or extension cord." He then jumps to his father's defense, telling me his father didn't hit him and tried to intervene when his mother was beating them. He then defends his mother as well. "She was drunk, though. She didn't know what she was doing. She tries to make up for it now. I forgive her." He tells me these days she's very supportive of him—sober for twenty-five years, she sends him money, writes to him, and allows him to stay at her home when he needs it.

During his original interview, Luke acknowledged he was molested on several occasions as a child by older men, beginning when he was eight. It's understandable how between that and the chaos and violence at home, Luke eventually began to get into trouble. When I asked him why he got into so many fights, he told me the fights were because he was picked on for being a quiet child. Furthermore, he never returned to school after his expulsion, attending a continuation school, where, he said, he attended special education classes: "I was just slow. It was hard for me to learn. I didn't have a lot of attention span."

While Luke's home life would be enough to explain why he might become a troublemaker in school, suffering from a learning disability without the understanding and accommodations he needed would have made learning especially difficult, frustrating, and even traumatic—thus, his acting out at school, and eventual failure, makes even more sense. Luke made a group of friends there who all sniffed paint together, and eventually he dropped out of school altogether, his life spiraling out of control for decades after.

In our meeting today, the hour goes by and he's emotional, insightful, and humble. I write it all down. Luke talks with pride about how he's stayed out of prison for almost a whole year this time. It's the longest he's been out of jail since he went in at fifteen.

"I got a real job," he says, smiling. "I have a car and it's registered, and I have insurance. I have a girlfriend, too. I've never had a relationship. She's real great. She's real attentive to me. And she has a great kid—a daughter. I teach her words from the dictionary. I'm getting used to being free."

Moved, I'm curious how far his newfound insight may reach. "What is your thinking today about your sexual crimes, Luke?" I ask him gently.

Luke looks down at his hands, then looks back up at me again, meeting my eyes. "I don't think that way toward anybody anymore. I have a girlfriend now, and sometimes when we're intimate if I hear something in her voice, I stop and ask, 'Are you okay?' I feel like what I did in the past when I was on drugs, I take responsibility, but it's not who I am." His voice cracks and he begins to cry again, wiping the tears aside.

It's clear he has learned a lot since we last met. I want to hear more. "How will you stay away from drugs and alcohol?"

"I don't use drugs anymore. I just say 'no.' I don't need the bullshit in my life. I don't need to hurt nobody. When I'm on drugs, I can't understand other people's feelings. I have NA now and a sponsor."

I nod. "And crime? How will you stay away from crime?"

He leans forward across the table in earnest. "I know now I need to watch out for things. Not just the big things, but I have to watch out for the small things, too."

"Right." Throughout this interview, I've been continually touched by his level of insight and accountability. No doubt he has a ways to go to understand why he has done what he's done—beyond the drugs—but the fact that he's taking responsibility and realizing the importance of his sobriety is meaningful. I nod and look up at him. "And what is your plan to not be charged with another sexual offense?"

Luke pauses for a moment and looks down at his hands in his lap. "I'm sorry about what I did. I used to do drugs to block out those things I did in the past. I did it because I was on drugs. It's not the drugs' fault, it's my fault, but I know without the drugs, I would never do those things."

"Where do you plan to be in five years?" Last time we met, he couldn't even imagine a month from then, let alone five years. I'm curious to see what he has to say today.

He smiles, excited to talk about the future. "My first goal is to get off parole." He pauses. "My second goal is to never hurt nobody in my whole life." His tears start up again. "I know it's never gonna happen again. I already gave thirty years of bad stuff, so I don't care if it takes thirty years to make it better. To make up for the hurt I did. I don't care if it takes my whole life."

By the time the interview is over, I'm deeply moved by the experience—by the obvious change in him. Every part of me wants to reverse my original decision—to send him back out in the world to continue to make a better life. But it doesn't matter what I want or don't want. It's my job to decide objectively. That feels hard today.

I leave the meeting feeling sad, knowing that his childhood and addiction have played a large part in who he has become. And while I'm moved by the changes he's made—his job, his newfound sobriety and accountability, his girlfriend and her child—I'm also aware these are only good starts.

Outside the prison, the world is so bright it hurts my eyes. My pupils adjust as I breathe in the fresh air and watch the leaves tremble in the breeze. I feel gratitude for the air and freedom I usually take for granted. On my drive home, I review the facts in my head and wrestle with the decision. Statistically, Luke is high risk. I know this without a doubt. His attachments are real and genuine, but they are as new as his sobriety. If Luke relapses on methamphetamines, his relationships with them won't keep him from offending again.

And yet I still feel for him. I feel sad for him, as I do for many of these guys facing indefinite lockup in a mental hospital. They have families and lives, and want to be free like the rest of us. Of course, unlike the rest of us, they repeatedly harm others. But most of these men still have the capacity to love and feel loss, and being locked up indefinitely is a terrible thought. I contemplate all of this as I drive another three-and-a-half hours back over the winding highways.

ONCE HOME, I'M QUICKLY IMMERSED in the routine of my family life—meditation, dinner with Josh and the kids, the details of everyone's day at work and school, doing dishes—and become a typical mom, who persistently nags her children toward bedtime. It's a relief to be back in the warm, loving, annoying humdrum routine of my daily life. I ask for a couple extra hugs from Josh and receive them.

"Tough day at the office?" he asks gently.

"Yeah. It was a hard one." My voice is muffled through his shoulder.

Luke's hope and tears stay with me, nagging at me. I'm grateful for what I have and simultaneously aware of what he doesn't have: Freedom. Stability. Longtime sobriety.

My good friend Steve—the one who's an expert on psychopaths—gets a little impatient with me when I talk about my sadness.

"It's not that I don't have empathy for those guys," he says, waving his hand in front of him for emphasis, "but these guys are hurting people. Creating victims. Even if violent criminals don't get less violent from serving time, at least if they're in prison we're safer from them."

I sigh. "True." I nod reluctantly. "I get that. If prison does nothing else, it prevents people who are violent from committing more violence on the rest of us."

He nods. "Exactly so. So I feel for them, but I don't feel sorry for them."

"I know. I don't feel sorry for them, either. People have to be held accountable. And I know that prison is the consequence for harming someone else. I get that."

He nods again.

"But, Steve, you know as well as I do that our criminal justice system is screwed up. It's selective—the poor and minorities are disproportionately represented—and a lot of people are in prison for crimes that aren't violent."

"I know, Sam. Believe me, I know. And there are people in prison who are wrongfully convicted. But we aren't talking about those people. That's not the work we do."

He's right, but it's difficult not to be saddened by these lives wasting away. When I think about these violent criminals, their own lives so often punctuated by addiction and violence, I recognize the traumatic experiences that shaped them, that pushed them down this road. I simply can't believe this is the best, most creative solution for the problem of crime.

The United States accounts for less than 5 percent of the world's population, but locks up nearly 20 percent of the world's prisoners. During the last two decades, state spending on prisons grew by 127 percent, six times the rate of spending on higher education. Something is clearly not working on a societal level.

I mull all of this over, and remind myself that at least in the hospital Luke and the others will be offered sex offender treatment. In prison there is nothing, and since he denies arousal to rape, I'm highly doubtful he would seek it out himself if he were released.

I'm going to give myself as much time as I can to weigh in on his case. I have a deadline, of course, but I want the emotional impact of our meeting to abate so I can approach the decision with as much objectivity as is required. I feel for Luke, and I want to support him, but these evaluations aren't just about Luke. They are about Luke's victims and potential future victims. They are about the law and an attempt to evaluate the situation as accurately as possible. An attempt to get at the meaning of "likely."

I shake my head. *Time to land here at home, honey.* I can't help thinking about Luke and his case, but gently try to refocus on the life in front of me. Sometimes it takes a while to transition home, to feel that my daily life is as real, as important, as the work I just left. Sometimes my daily life seems so small and insignificant—what we should have for dinner, how Eva and Rachel did on their history test, or how a boy was unkind to Kye at school.

It seems so trivial in comparison to the decision about Luke facing indefinite commitment to a mental institution. But I know that my life, and the lives of Josh and my children, are no less important. Each day may be minor on its own, but added together, they create a whole life lived.

I take deep breaths to shift focus and know that if I didn't have a solid meditation practice to root me, to bring me back into myself and my world, I would certainly want a drink to try to unwind and let the day go. In spite of a lack of interest in alcohol for many years, there was a time when I tried having a drink or two when I came home from these interviews, to blur the edges of work and leave it behind. It kind of worked for a month or two. Josh would join me for drinks and I could feel myself relax as he relaxed with me, both softened by alcohol. Ultimately, though, I found that it didn't really change things. It simply made me tired and less clear, and any time we might have argued, it became much worse. I was blurring out my day at prison, but I was also blurring out my evening at home, missing out on the stuff that really mattered to me.

So I stopped drinking again and went back to meditating. Meditating takes more time and discipline than drinking, but once I'm there, TM takes no effort. It simply releases the stresses of the day and gives me an experience of deep rest. I emerge more clear and present. Slowly my mind stops sorting and thinking and working so hard, and I'm liberated into the rest of my life.

Chapter 8

DREAMS AND NIGHTMARES

AFTER A SHORT TIME IN THE FIELD of psychology, I discovered that my work didn't take place solely in the realm of my waking life. My unconscious mind was quietly working away under the surface as well. Early on in my career, I was providing treatment for sex offenders and there was a man in the treatment program, Mike, who in the beginning was very challenging to get a handle on. At times he seemed psychopathic—manipulative, scary when angry, his past filled with violence and intensity. In one group session, he told us that when his high-school girlfriend broke up with him, he refused to accept it.

"I was so angry," he shared matter-of-factly. "Why would she break up with me? Things were great; then she just up and ended it."

There were nods around the room. Most people who have been in high school can relate to the feelings of anger and disappointment from a sudden, unwanted breakup.

"I just couldn't handle it." He shrugs, looking around the room.

"What did you do to get through it?" I ask. "Maybe there were ways you learned to cope then, that you can use now?"

He smiled broadly. "I don't think so." He shook his head. "At the time, I just refused to let her end it. One day after school, I made her get into my car, took her home, and tied her up in my basement. I kept her there for hours before I finally let her go. I just refused to accept it."

The room was silent. No one was nodding now. I blinked a few times.

"Right," I eventually replied evenly. "Not the way you want to cope now." The room breathed again as everyone shifted in their seats and we moved on, but I took note.

Mike was a former boxer and U.S. Marine, and had remained a muscular and powerful man. He was practiced at the art of intimidation, and often his responses to others seemed slippery, elusive, and hard to read, but everyone still listened closely. He looked around the room, but never made eye contact. He had our attention, even when he was sitting, doing nothing.

At other times, however, the therapists in the program were impressed by his participation and how he appeared to have empathy and connection with other members. He progressed through treatment, and completed what was asked of him. He did his homework. He participated in groups. He shared a great deal about himself and could be charming. He always seemed respectful toward me and listened to what I and others had to say.

When Mike had first come into the program, he was asked—as all members were—to share his offense with the group. He said he'd had sex with his teenage stepdaughter. He implied it was "consensual."

"She was very attractive," he explained. "Mature for her age. We kind of fell into it." The therapists and group members all worked under that premise for a couple of months. Even though, of course, the action is illegal and harmful for the stepdaughter—and, in effect, can't possibly be truly consensual, there is a difference between using force and something that might feel "consensual" for the teen. *They'd just fallen into it.* His conviction was for sex with a minor, so it was almost plausible.

But a couple of months into the time Mike was in treatment, I had a dream that made me understand a statement by David Dow in *The Autobiography of an Execution.* In it, Dow writes eloquently about his experiences as a lawyer who specialized in capital punishment cases. He hauntingly reports, "I write down my dreams because they scare me. They scare me because I understand them."

In my dream, Mike got up in the middle of group therapy, strode across the center of the group, and picked me up with my arms pinned to my side. I fought with him as he unflinchingly overpowered me and tore off my clothes. I woke up in the dark with my heart pounding, shaken. The rest of the night, I tossed and turned, the experience too real to shake.

The next day at the office, I went directly to Mike's file and read carefully through the police reports. I was somehow not surprised to find that he had raped his stepdaughter. The shock wasn't that he had lied, it was more that we hadn't questioned it sooner. His story had been believable and his manner seductive. Those of us who do this work never assume we're getting the whole story, or even the true story. And yet here we were, taken in for several months.

We normally read through the files carefully, but somehow this one had slipped through. Not only was it without "consent," but he'd actually told her he would kill the girl's mother (his wife) if the girl refused to do what he said. The case had been reduced to sex with a minor as part of a plea agreement. He was confronted, of course, but always wiggled out of any accountability. He was slippery and dangerous, and determined to remain so.

Ever since that experience, I've been determined to respect my unconscious mind, aware that there are times when it knows more than I do. A quiet part of me had paid attention, and refused to be seduced by him. I have always listened to that part of me since. Just because some guy seems "easy to be with," or open, or making progress, it doesn't mean I'm getting the whole story. It's possible even Luke, who seems to be genuinely making progress, could be not entirely forthcoming. I base my decisions on the facts that are before me, and the statistical analysis, but I also never stop listening to the still, quiet place inside me.

———

Sometimes my dreams are simply a reminder of the effect this work has on my psyche. Most of the time, I can read the hundreds of police reports of sexual violence with some detachment.

Compartmentalizing what I'm exposed to, approaching it with a scientific mind, and having a lot of experience and exposure all help in that regard. But I'm not completely unaffected and would never want to be; I've always thought that if I got to that point—unaffected—it would be time to quit. Rather than becoming unaffected, it's more that I've become practiced at keeping a distance from it.

I can't seem to do this with violent movies, but when it's work, I can keep it at arm's length. Why this difference, I find hard to explain. I just know that while I can read police reports and talk about violent acts, seeing it depicted graphically in the movies is something I simply can't tolerate.

One time in the car, I heard an interview on the NPR show *Fresh Air* with a journalist— C.J. Chivers—who has covered war and conflict. He said that he lives in a house without a TV—hasn't had one for years. That he doesn't want to see any violence outside of his job. When asked why that was, he said, "It's different when you're covering it. You have a reason. You have a purpose, you have a job, and you have training. And you follow your training." He went on to say that violence isn't entertaining for him, it's frightening, and he'd prefer not to be frightened at home.

I relate deeply to this. I find graphic depictions where I'm simply a passive observer to be disturbing and not at all entertaining. But usually when I have a job to do, I can hear or read the stories and not take them completely in. I just do my job.

Oddly, I find my work with perpetrators less challenging in some ways than working with trauma survivors. Of course, I feel deeply for the victim, it's why I'm doing the work. But when working directly with the victim the trauma is alive in the room. It's re-experienced in the telling. With a perpetrator, or a police report, the trauma happened somewhere else. To someone else.

This is the one thing that allows me to generally hold my own in this work, not allowing it to get to me. But every now and then, a story sneaks through my professional defenses and punches me in the gut. It's not always the saddest or most tragic story, or even the most brutal. To be honest, I don't always know what allows it to happen.

Today the story that has snuck under my guard is this police report: A twelve-year-old girl goes for a car ride with her uncle at night. Two men she doesn't know join them. It's late, and the young girl dozes off in the car while they're driving around. When she wakes up, the uncle is gone. The men take her to an unfamiliar house and force her to get undressed; she refuses at first, but they hit her until she does. She has trouble getting her leotard off, so they cut it off. They rape her.

This story is terrible. It's terrible in the usual way that rapes of children are, their innocence being taken from them in such a brutal way. And the detail of her leotard sparks an even deeper grief in me, thinking of her as a young dancer, and the fact that my own twelve-year-old daughter Rachel is a dancer.

But it's the other part of the story that really gets to me: that of the betrayal by her uncle. It dawns on me as I'm reading the police report that the uncle probably had a debt of some sort to pay and left his niece for these two men as payment. The girl is not only raped by strangers, but betrayed by someone she knows and trusts. She fell asleep because she trusted she was safe. But she wasn't.

As I read this report, I do not feel detached. Even after, I feel nauseous, haunted, and enraged.

That night, in my dream, I'm in a giant mansion wandering from room to room. I open a door and a man runs up to me. "I just have to find someone to celebrate with!" He smiles wide and claps his hands with a bang.

My chest balls into a fist and my breath catches. *Where are my children?* Somehow, I know this man is not safe. I start running through the mansion. *I have to find them before he does!* I'm frantically searching, but can't find them anywhere. My heart is pounding and my eyes are wild as I run through room after room, until I finally throw open a door and discover them in bed with him. My heart falls straight down my legs and into the floor as I walk in, laser focused on the scene in front of me, my veins on fire. I can see he's showing them what his genitals look like. I feel I will beat him to death or choke him with my bare hands.

"Get away from them!" I scream at the top of my lungs, and lunge toward them, waking myself with a jolt, my voice hoarsely crying out in the quiet. The room is stifling hot and I'm dripping with sweat; I realize Josh and I accidentally left the heat on during the night. The sheets and blankets are twisted around me; I feel bound, trapped. I'm deeply disturbed, agitated, and angry—angry about all the children, betrayed and abused.

———

THE NEXT MORNING, I'm in the kitchen helping with lunches, getting everyone ready. My body has calmed, of course, but I'm still a little shaken. As I'm focusing on the task at hand, as usual I don't get to see the first part of Kye's morning wake-up, where they stretch, roll over, and try to stay asleep even as the morning light and hustle-bustle of a school day force them up. Or where they climb down the ladder from their loft, carefully and carelessly all at once, and wander through the bedroom and kitchen. It's here where I come across them, in the hallway or the kitchen, their hair mussed from sleep, their voice rough from a whole night unused.

"I have to go to the bathroom," they explain, quietly and shyly, looking down and away.

"Yes, yes, of course, go ahead, cutie," I say.

They scurry into the bathroom to stand at the toilet, emptying the night's bladder. And then they're done. Leaving the bathroom, they find me and look up into my face, arms open and up, and I bend down and scoop them up, lifting them off the floor as I straighten. I breathe deeply through my nose and inhale the familiar smell of sleep and child and soft that I've been smelling since their birth and has become more familiar to me than almost any other.

They squeeze me tightly, and I wrap my arms around them and squeeze back. If I hold them a moment longer, I know they will wrap their legs tightly around me, too. *This is heaven,* I think, *a place where nothing else matters for a moment.* Our hearts pressed together, breathing in and out, smiling into each other's hair.

As the morning progresses and I'm joined in the kitchen by Eva and Rachel, I'm startled as I glance over at them; every time I blink, they're looking and acting more like teens and less like girls. Both are almost as tall as me, Eva with her soulful green eyes and Rachel's browns that twinkle when she smiles. Even though the change has been gradual, and I already know we've entered the world of pop songs, social life, and cool clothing, it still feels sudden that they're done with imaginary games, fun art projects, and playing with their younger sibling. I have been expecting it and still I'm completely unprepared. They have been great kids and I love the young women they're becoming, but did it have to happen so fast?

I don't admit this to anyone aloud because it sounds strange to say it, but I'm thrilled and relieved they have made it out of early childhood still "untouched" and left to evolve sexually at their own pace and curiosity. Thank God they haven't been molested. But now we are facing a new world of danger—the world of adolescence. It's the world of boys and men who will find them beautiful and irresistible and will want to possess them. Of men like Luke, who break into homes and take whatever they want, including the women in them.

My twins are blossoming and lovely, and I have even less ability to protect them now than I used to. They're more independent, more exposed, more left to their own devices. All I can do is educate them and keep lines of communication open and hope for the best. Hope in spite of everything I know.

Part Three

PERMEABLE

He who fights with monsters should look to it that he himself does not become a monster. When you gaze long into an abyss, the abyss also gazes into you.

—Friedrich Nietzsche

Chapter 9

CHOICES

I'VE SPENT THE WEEK IN DEEP AMBIVALENCE about Luke Miller's second evaluation. I call his parole agent, who has also felt moved by this man's efforts. He believes that Luke is, in fact, "really trying" to turn his life around. He genuinely seems to have become a different person than the man I met before.

When I asked Luke if he understands why breaking into homes and raping women is wrong, he had replied earnestly, "It's invading their privacy. When I do meth, I have no regard for people's property and safety. I make totally wrong decisions. That's why I need to stop using drugs."

Wanting to see if he was capable of more than that, I replied, "Okay, Luke, but what do you think the impact is on those women? How do you think it affects them?"

He paused for a long minute, gathering his thoughts before replying, "Putting myself in their shoes, probably scared, hurt. It's an invasion of their privacy." He paused again. "They might have felt they were going to die. Worthless. Afraid of men after."

All of that is impressive—I was touched by his efforts of empathy at the time. But he could understand those things, and even feel them, and still not be able to control his actions moving forward. Prior evaluations report that he has a history of lying and manipulation, and he has admitted to it. Even in this second evaluation, I discover he's still lying about some things. He had a relapse when he told me he had stayed clean, and he had a harder time holding a job and finding stable housing than he had let on.

Since the age of eleven, he has never been able to maintain sobriety or stay out of prison. And while he only has one qualifying conviction, there are three reports of his breaking into homes and attempting to rape women. Documented fantasies and arousal to raping women. Even after repeated arrests and convictions, he continued to repeat the pattern, and the presence of children in the home did not dissuade him. So the question is not: Is he changing? The question is: Can we bank on the recent changes? He has been out of prison and sober for the longest time in his adult life. But it's only been eight months. Eight months doesn't change the statistics or the risk level. It's simply too short of a time.

Because I feel sad for him and believe, like his parole agent, that his efforts to turn his life around are genuine, I send my evaluation to a colleague who's conservative with diagnoses and thinks critically about these decisions, insisting that perpetrators meet the criteria fully. He sends it back with a note: *Strong evaluation. Looks solid.*

I consult with other trusted colleagues. They listen carefully, then speak the facts back to me: This man has a history of admitting to arousal at the thought of raping women; has attempted to rape several women; has a diverse criminal history, beginning at the age of eleven; has an addiction to methamphetamines; and, basically, meets the criteria pretty clearly. They reaffirm what I know—that even though he has been making efforts to turn his life around in the past year, we cannot make assumptions about someone's future behavior based on so short a time of current behavior. In some ways, Luke's recent efforts don't matter: In reality he might indeed be lower risk, but statistically we can't draw that conclusion based on only eight months—or even a year—out of prison. He just hasn't had enough time in the community for me to be confident he's changed. A part of me was hoping my colleagues would find my arguments weak or that I should change my original decision, but I read it through once more and must agree—even with the new research, he still meets the criteria. I cannot argue them out of it, nor, eventually, can I argue myself out of it.

I deeply long to support Luke's first try at acting like a citizen, but forty pages later, I submit my report that he meets the SVP criteria for indefinite involuntary hospitalization. A few days later, I get an email stating that the case is being referred to the DA; the other evaluator concluded he met the criteria as well.

I feel miserable. It's not that I don't get it—on paper, the law was designed to capture someone like him. He gets high on methamphetamines and breaks into a woman's home to rape her, gets incarcerated, comes out, and does it again. Over and over, he gets out of prison and harms others. As a society, we want to protect our citizens from someone who repeatedly harms them.

But sadly for him, that means loss of freedom and loss of family. Loss of a chance to create the new life he was longing for. A new life he had started, for the first time, and was hopeful he could succeed at it. Instead, now he sits in jail awaiting a trial, facing indefinite incarceration.

At times like this, I question where the balance lies between the imperfect science of prevention and personal freedom. Is it possible Luke will never harm another person? Possible, but not likely if he doesn't continue the major changes in his life, and there's no guarantee he will. Relapse could happen any time. There's no way to predict the future with certainty. All I have is his past behavior, and statistics based on studies. His history includes the fact that he keeps getting out of prison and victimizing more people. Society, civil liberties, punishment, prevention, "likely."

———————

THE NEXT DAY, I'M GRUMPY. Could be Luke's case, could be life, could be I woke up on the wrong side of the bed, but I find myself irritated at everyone and everything. Early evening we sit down as a family to meditate before dinner and suddenly I'm aware of Josh's physical presence next to me. I'm overwhelmed with a desire to hug him and just to forget about everything—the irritation, the anger, the hard day—to just sink into his arms and cuddle together.

As the desire for this loving contact washes over me, I observe it and think: *This is it, isn't it?*

Everyone longs for this sometimes—the desire to just wash away what is sad, uncomfortable, painful. To just get away from all those feelings and sink into something familiar and comforting, pleasurable and soothing. For some, it's certain foods that might give them that feeling; for others, it may be a favorite song. For me, Josh is that familiar, soothing thing. I met him when I was just shy of twenty; his hugs and loving embrace have been present and providing me comfort and pleasure for over twenty years. We all can relate to that feeling of wanting to lose ourselves in the pleasure.

For sex offenders, unfortunately, the pathway to pleasure and losing oneself is to the detriment of self and/or others.

Chapter 10

TRIAL

FOR THREE DAYS, ON AND OFF, I prepare to testify in a case in Stockton that has gone to trial. A part of me always has mixed feelings about a case going to trial. On the one hand, it means two expert evaluators and the DA have all agreed this person is compelled to commit more violent sex offenses, is at high risk for doing it again, and should go to treatment rather than being released back into our communities. Society is ostensibly safer for it.

Personally, it means I will have to subject myself to the intensely acrimonious courtroom testimony that's part of this work. It's here my role shifts from evaluator to expert witness. I testify for hours or even days as the defense attorney picks through my report, questioning every statement, every assumption, every conclusion. On the rare occasion that I'm an evaluator who has come to the minority conclusion, it will be the prosecution who is taking apart my report. Either way, every attempt will be made to discredit the work I've done and cast doubt on me as a professional. Even my personal life must be beyond reproach.

Of course, working with serious sex offenders means that my home address has special hidden status with the DMV, and I'm extremely careful about what is online/accessible regarding myself and my family. But as an expert witness, my life as a whole must be immaculate. My social media presence is small, innocuous, reveals little, and is set to private. My tattoos are hidden. Little, if anything, is public about my political point of view, finances, or personal life. My conduct in public and on the web is always professional and impeccable. This work is not just about the work; it governs much of my life.

Of course, that's how it should be. Everyone has a right to the best possible defense, and the stakes for these individuals are incredibly high: They face indeterminate confinement. Confronting this intense testimony is part of what forces me to be as certain as possible of my conclusions when I write my evaluation. Personally, it places powerful limitations on how I conduct myself, but I have a tendency to be very private anyway, so I can live with it.

Some of my colleagues find trial testimony an exciting challenge. "Bring it on," my friend and colleague Martin says. "I welcome it."

I, on the other hand, am filled with dread each time I have to prepare for a trial. Not because I'm a particularly anxious person; in fact, I'm generally quite calm, and once on the stand, I give clear, composed, and accessible testimony. Nor has it anything to do with my qualifications—I have extensive knowledge and experience, and every court has approved me as an expert.

It's that having my professional work (and, at times, personal life) questioned and torn apart for hours in a court of law is, for me, an intense and unpleasant experience. And being an introvert by nature doesn't help. The process leaves me exhausted, and the whole process takes over my life while it's happening. Each time I prepare to testify, I never feel ready, despite having memorized the facts, statistics, research, and psychological aspects of each case, and discovering each time, upon testifying, that I have prepared well enough and am undoubtedly an expert in the field. Still, it's a bit of a relief when the result of an evaluation is negative and I don't have to subject myself to the pressure, intensity, and grueling nature of a trial.

In the Stockton case, I have found the inmate to meet the criteria, so I'll be an expert witness for the district attorney. The man has a history of breaking into women's homes and raping whomever he finds there, and while he denies all of it, the convictions keep coming. As an expert, I cannot bring any notes to the stand with me, so I have memorized all the details of the case, crimes, and relevant research. I organize everything into notebooks, with tabs and separators. I review all of the research that may apply. I pace through the house, cross-examining myself in my head and working hard to answer the questions out loud in a simple, clear way. I remind myself, again and again, to take deep breaths and just keep studying the case, relevant research and statistics, and reviewing my decision.

The morning of the trial, I wake up and force breakfast into my stomach. By the time my suit is on, I've taken several trips to the toilet—whenever I'm anxious, my bowels get me ready for battle. I drive two hours to Stockton, and even this beautiful spring day can't break me out of my focused state. I arrive, park, and stride into the courthouse. On my way in, the officer screening bags tells me I need to throw away a fork that I had forgotten about in my bag—evidently, it's a potential weapon.

After I've waited a bit, the DA comes to meet me. As we walk toward the courtroom, he briefs me on how the case has been going. "It's been a circus," he says loudly. "The man arrogantly damns himself with his own testimony."

I nod and listen half-attentively as we walk into the courtroom, and soon I'm on the stand, being sworn in by a kind presiding judge, while the jury, attorneys, inmate, and his family all watch.

For the next four hours, I answer every question asked of me to the best of my knowledge and ability. Testifying takes more focus and concentration than any other aspect of my job as I listen to the exact wording of each question asked, and attempt to answer as precisely and accurately as I can. I only have to testify every couple of months, but when I do, it's intense.

When the DA questions me, his goal is to help me be clear and to lay out my report so that everything lines up, makes sense, and my argument is supported. He has brought this case to trial because of the reports I, and the second psychologist, wrote. We represent his case, so he wants it to be strong. But when the defense attorney questions me, her goal is the opposite—to cast as much doubt as possible on everything I have to say.

"Dr. Stein," she says at one point, waving some papers in the air, "have you read this recent paper by Dr. Hanson on recidivism rates?"

"I'm sure I have," I reply calmly. "Do you want to tell me which paper it is, and did you have a question about it?"

"It's important, isn't it, Dr. Stein, that someone in your position keeps up with the latest research?" she asks smugly, raising her eyebrows, still holding papers in the air.

"Absolutely," I reply. "It's crucial to our job."

"Well, you must have been aware, then, that his findings cast some doubt on your conclusions," she says, lowering the paper for emphasis.

"I'm actually not aware of that," I say firmly. "Can you please explain your statement?"

She refers to numbers and statistics, and I counter with my own reasoning. So far, she hasn't thrown anything at me that I haven't already thought about, but there's no guarantee that will continue to be the case. Usually, when I testify, I'm prepared enough. Every now and then, I'm blindsided. Her main goal is, of course, to cast doubt on my abilities. Even the way she poses her questions is designed to shoot holes in my credibility.

No matter how cool it is in the courtroom, drops of sweat slowly trace the middle of my back. I keep my face impassive as I'm forced to defend every statement and conclusion I've made in my report. I must also be ready and willing to acknowledge all of the weaknesses and "gray areas" of the assessment; it's not bulletproof. No assessment on a human being could be.

"Can you say, without a doubt, that this man will commit another sex offense?" she asks me, looking me straight in the eyes.

"No, I can't," I reply, my voice even. "I can only speak about

which category of reoffenders he's most similar to. In his case, it's high risk."

Regardless of what question I'm answering, I have to be crystal clear, to the non-psychologist and psychologist alike. It's intense, grueling, exhausting, powerful, and at times exhilarating. It is as it should be; this is an incredibly weighty process and no stone should be left unturned. Lives are in the balance.

During a brief break, I walk down the long hallway outside the courtroom and think about how weird and heavy this whole thing is—the victims, the man who is facing indefinite hospitalization, me up on the stand as an expert—and then I'm back on the stand, deeply in concentration.

We break for lunch and I'm taken by the DA and his assistant to a cheap Chinese restaurant with greasy food. We talk about the case. "Really, this guy should be fried for the things he's done," he says between mouthfuls. He is fully confident in his decision to prosecute a guy who counts among his victims both a teenager and a woman in her late seventies. Although I'm confident in my decision that he meets the criteria, I'm never 100 percent certain of anything in life, and his comments about the electric chair make me uncomfortable. I nod and say nothing.

After lunch I return to the stand. For the rest of my testimony, nothing else exists—no other thoughts, feelings, people—only this one place, time, and the question being asked of me in that moment. Sometimes I feel relaxed, confident, and connected to the process and my own store of knowledge. Other times I feel badgered, harassed, and frustrated. And no matter how warm or cool the room is, I'm clammy. Always I'm concentrating—the court stenographer typing every word I say.

Then it's done. The prosecution rests, and so does the defense. The judge thanks me and I am excused. I find myself breathing deeply again, back in my car, driving home. I'm slightly euphoric; the judge's assistant has told me it was some of the best expert testimony she has seen in ten years—that I was clear, thoughtful, and to the point. An attorney-in-training thanked me for how much she learned. Most of all, though, I'm relieved it's over and done.

When I once described the experience of testifying to a friend, she enthusiastically compared me to Arjuna, the great warrior of the Bhagavad Gita. "It is so powerfully single-pointed," she said. "You keep your eye on the truth as best as you can understand it, no matter what, because lives are truly at stake. It's like a spiritual path. It's like your life's purpose, your journey toward enlightenment."

I pondered her statement. Of course, I would love to consider myself akin to Arjuna—in conversation with God and aligning my efforts with dharma, or righteousness, on my path toward self-realization. But grandiose aspirations aside, she was right, perhaps, in some small sense. There is a battle within me on each of these cases—a battle with all of my own doubts, fears, thoughts, experiences—to find the truest course possible. And perhaps there is something spiritual about it: finding the true course that allows me to synthesize all I know, speak only what I believe to be true and ethical, and move forward without attachment to the outcome.

Then again, maybe I'm more like Buzz Lightyear, battling imaginary aliens.

By the time I get home, there is only white noise where my brain used to be. It's as if my brain has been rewired for the purpose of listening, focusing, and picking apart every word and sentence. But now I'm simply exhausted, as if I cannot have another thought of my own if I tried.

I strip off my suit and take a shower. The warm water is tangible, offering me relief—nothing to be deciphered or analyzed; it's just soothing water. I put on comfortable clothes and sit down to meditate and slowly descend back into my body, but even after the deep rest, it's difficult for me to completely unwind or to experience my brain as mine again.

I'm exhausted and out of it and want someone else to take care of everything. I want to just sit and do nothing. But Josh tells me he has to work late, as he's in the middle of trying to write code for his software program. The kids need dinner and help with homework. Kye is coughing and saying their stomach hurts. I force myself to do what needs to be done, and going through the motions, I slowly, slowly, melt into me again.

TWO DAYS LATER, IT'S SUNDAY—family yoga day. I'm looking forward to getting further out of my mind and into my body, and sharing the practice with my family, but Eva is angry. "I'm tired," she says, coming into the room where I'm getting ready. "I just want to stay home and hang out." Not being in control can be challenging for her.

"I know that feeling," I reply sympathetically, "but you have to come anyway." Josh and I are firm about everyone participating in Sunday yoga.

Eva's anger flares. "I don't want to go!" Then, "Mommy, is college age seventeen?"

"Eighteen," I answer. "Why?"

"Because," she yells, storming out, "I'm counting down the days!"

I'm taken aback at the sting of it, then chuckle at the juxtaposition of the sweetness of her youthful name for me—"Mommy"—with her angry declaration of independence.

Eva hears my chuckle. "It's not funny!" she yells from the other room, and I tell her I agree, it's not. Her frustration and helplessness are palpable.

I like to give my kids choices and freedom. No child wants to be told what to do, and giving them choices and freedom recognizes their humanity as independent people. But sometimes, as their parent, my job is to *not* give them choice—to insist they go to school, brush their teeth, and be kind, even if they don't feel like it. Because it helps instill good values and good habits, and because it's what they need. As a parent, I'm charged with making that determination.

I have often thought about men on parole and their relationship with their parole agent in these same terms—in some ways, when people are on parole, they are back to having a parent again. They are being told what they can and cannot do, and their life is overseen by the agent. I can only imagine how it chafes. How challenging it must be to be grown and be treated like a child again.

All of this makes me think about years ago when I worked in a group home for severely abused children who had been taken from their parents. They were so disturbed from early abuse, they had become abusive toward themselves and others and couldn't be maintained in foster homes. They had to be watched, contained, and constantly worked with.

For their safety, the doors between the dining area, bedrooms, and school were all locked, with only the adults in possession of the keys. One day I picked up a newly arrived child for therapy—he was not only a new arrival, but new to life in a locked facility. He ran ahead of me and reached for the doorknob, as anyone would, only to find it locked. Realizing it was locked, he waited for me to come up and unlock it. During his first few weeks at the facility, this happened each time I came to get him. But I remember the day vividly when he no longer reached for the doorknob. Like the men who go from prison, where they have no choice, to parole, where they have little, he had become institutionalized. He had lost the experience of agency over his own life.

———————

THE FOLLOWING MORNING, I start my week awake before dawn. Josh wakes briefly to say a sleepy goodbye, and I scoot out of the house while everyone else is still asleep. At the airport, I feel oddly out of place with no luggage. After a quick flight on a very small, loud plane, I find myself in Humboldt County, farther north than my prior visit, where it's quiet and insanely beautiful.

Everywhere redwoods stand like too many kings for one kingdom, and there are as many cows as trees gathered around streams and rivers. It's as if the whole place sprang up just to be gorgeous. As I drive the highways toward the institution, I again struggle to find a way to take photos that speak of the ugly, colorless world I'm about to enter.

I'm visiting a jail today, rather than a prison. A prison is a state or federal institution where convicted offenders serve longer sentences. A jail is a local, short-term holding facility for the newly arrested, those awaiting trial or sentencing, or those sentenced to serve less than a year. The man I'm interviewing today has violated his parole, so he has briefly gone to jail.

Once I pass security, I have the incredibly odd experience of a voice directing me from above. It kicks in when I first go past security into the jail and feel lost. I stand there befuddled, realizing there are no signs, and I don't have any sort of map. The fluorescent lights buzz overhead, and it could be night or day. I look down the hallway to the right, then the left, and it all looks the same: white walls, gray floor, leading to more hallways.

Suddenly a male voice says, "Take the elevators in front of you to the third floor."

Startled, I look around, and then look up to see speakers in the corner. I don't see a camera, but I assume he can see me.

"Okay," I say, "thanks," not at all sure whether he can also hear me. I get off the elevator on the third floor; and before I have time to register that I'm still lost, the voice says, "Turn right and proceed down the hallway."

He gives me directions until I get to the meeting room. His voice is kind, helpful, and professional, but being monitored at every turn makes me anxious and self-conscious as I wind my way through the concrete, windowless white-gray hallways. It's like driving next to a police car; even if I'm obeying all the traffic laws, I'm certain I'll be caught doing something wrong. I feel like a kid. My mouth is dry. The air smells used. It's not lost on me that everyone here is monitored to this degree.

Once at my destination, I morph into a grown-up again, in my button-down shirt and dress pants. I interview a man who appears nothing like his file suggests. Luis has a history of various sex offenses—child molestation, indecent exposure, and sexual harassment. But once I meet this "sex-crazed repeat offender," he turns out to be an awkward, aging man with a difficult childhood.

"I didn't speak until I was five," he says, "and didn't make complete sentences until I was ten."

"School must have been challenging for you," I invite him to continue.

"I got into fights with other kids all the time. I didn't fit in. I hated it. It was like spending a day in hell."

"Did you have any friends?"

He pauses before answering. "I had one friend at a time . . . They wouldn't be that great of a friend, they'd be just a part-time friend."

I ask him if he'd ever received a diagnosis to explain his difficulties.

"I just found out that in third grade I was diagnosed as extremely dyslexic and extremely autistic. That explains a lot. I've really struggled all my life; I'm just now getting to where I have communication skills and people understand me. I'm a loner, basically. I'm outwardly standoffish, inwardly emotional."

Later, when I ask him if he understands why child molestation is illegal, he says, "Yes, it mentally damages them. I learned about it from my counselor . . . I just don't pick up on things." He looks down at his hands. I look down at my notes and write. The interview goes on this way. Each of his offenses seemed to be related to his extreme difficulty knowing how to make a human connection, and inability to read the experiences of others.

"What about this child molestation conviction? What happened there?"

His head hangs as he looks into his hands on his lap. He doesn't look up to answer. "I was young then. Just barely a teenager. I know now it was wrong. I know now I hurt that kid. But at the time, I didn't know how to connect with other kids. I didn't know how to be close to them. The kids my age—I didn't know how to be part of that scene. I was more comfortable around younger kids."

"I see. So you were trying to be close to that kid?"

"Yeah. I thought it might be okay." He still doesn't lift his head.

"What about this indecent exposure?"

He lets out a long, deep sigh and finally raises his head to look at me. "It's the same thing with that one and the sexual harassment. Those were ladies at work . . . that I worked with. Different jobs, but the same kind of thing. I know this sounds stupid, but both times I thought it was a mutual thing. I thought maybe we could date each other." He spreads his hands, palms up, then lets them fall again. "When I look back on it now, I can see how stupid it was. But that's how I was thinking at the time." He looks down at his lap again. "I feel really bad I upset those women. That I scared them."

A list of crimes versus an actual person. Even after all these years, I can still be guilty of reading about what a person has done and imagining I'm going out to meet a monster. What a shock to discover, once again, it's just an ordinary person sitting across from me. I feel no fear sitting there; instead, my heart is heavy with sadness.

I suppose there's comfort in thinking about someone who commits terrible acts as something other than human. Some kind of scary "other being," something other than what I am. But if I don't see myself in this person, then I will never live in the truth of what it means to be human. I know God is often a loaded concept for people, and many won't agree with me when I say this, but for me, God is nature. God is the world, the universe, and everything in it, but more than that, God is evolution—every natural thing is constantly evolving, adapting, growing, and changing. If I deny any part of that, I won't be able to see all of what God is—both the beauty and ugliness. The humanity of my own struggles and every-one else's. I'll be diminished. I'll stay small and fearful of "those people out there." My heart will never be big enough to take in all of what God is.

Most people really do want to lead a good life. When people say, "Children aren't born bad," that's actually true in almost all cases. Even kids who are mean or bullies, self-centered or manipulative, who seem to care little for the feelings of others, when you peel back the top layer, a wound festers. Given the chance, that wound will heal and the child will become someone different. Someone who has compassion and longs for love and connection. The impulse for evolution is right there.

So it is also with adults. It may take longer, but I've found time and time again that if I give a criminal, a bully, or an addict who doesn't trust a soul a chance to slowly build trust, it will begin to form. If I show up authentically and with clear boundaries and true compassion, glimmers of empathy and kindness start to poke through the anger. Warmth eventually turns into a relationship. Over time, with patience and perseverance, the hard defensive shell is chipped away as the opportunity for connection knocks again and again. I believe it's what we all long for: genuine connection. I don't know if it was real or sustainable with Luke, but it seemed he had gotten a genuine start in this process. It's moving to see when it happens.

Of course, there are those rare exceptions: The seven-year-old kid who tortures an animal simply to see what will happen. The twelve-year-old girl who organizes her friends to torment a girl in her class because it might be interesting to see when she breaks. The nine-year-old who shrugs and says, "Because I wanted to," when asked why he's just beaten a five-year-old neighbor kid. Not out of anger, rage, envy, powerlessness, or acting out pain, but because the thought simply occurred to him as he watched the young child idly draw in chalk on the sidewalk in front of their house and he wanted to see what it would be like.

As adults, people like this don't always appear cold or angry. They can even be quite charming and funny . . . until they're not.

They have no desire to love or trust, only to build trust when it's useful to them.

In *Without Conscience: The Disturbing World of the Psychopaths Among Us*, author Robert Hare describes psychopathy this way: "Psychopaths are social predators who charm, manipulate, and ruthlessly plow their way through life, leaving a broad trail of broken hearts, shattered expectations, and empty wallets. Completely lacking in conscience and in feelings for others, they selfishly take what they want and do as they please."

There is no known treatment for someone like this. Like Joe. There are no wounds to heal, no longing for any connection to grab hold of. Every time you reach out to touch, to connect, there's only a momentary feeling of a grip, before your hands are slipping and sliding and suddenly you're standing without the floor beneath you. Like when a wave tumbles you over and over, and for a moment you don't know which way the air is, and you stare at this person and try to remember who you are and which thought was your own . . . and feel afraid. For this person, treatment consists only of figuring out a way to convince them that it's in their own best interest not to harm any more people.

But most people aren't like that. Even criminals who've used and abused others have histories filled with physical abuse as children, learning disorders, and a failed education system, and/or families who taught them how to steal and pimp. These men, like Luke, aren't without conscience, or beyond help, if they ever open themselves to the possibility of change. They're men with deep pain and shame, who need help. For themselves and for the rest of us.

After a couple of hours with Luis, the interview is over and I'm back in the tiny airport, waiting for the tiny plane, struck by how surreal it feels to go back to everyday life after leaving the prison. It's always such a powerful juxtaposition: the "inside" of bare walls, concrete, steel, uniforms, prison wear, rules, order, no color with the exception of the orange jumpsuit, no smells except for cafeteria food and cleaner, no sound except for voices and doors; versus the "outside," where there's sunlight, fresh air, wind, color, smells of flowers, exhaust, and rain; there's music, and people of all genders and ages.

I always long for a hug when I leave. And I find walking out of an institution a little overwhelming and makes my heart hurt—there's so much trauma inside those walls. I feel at a distance from everyone else who has not experienced life "inside." I can't imagine what it would be like to walk out after twenty years instead of four hours.

Chapter 11

CONTINUUM

A WEEK LATER, I GET AN EMAIL from the DA on the case that involved my testimony in Stockton. There is nothing in the body of the email except for a newspaper article reporting that the man in question was found to meet SVP criteria by the jury and was being sent to Coalinga State Hospital with an indeterminate sentence.

I had received a phone message from the DA's assistant as the jury finished their deliberation. "We're very pleased with your testimony," the assistant's voicemail said. "The jury had a challenging time with the decision, but they said your testimony about the case was clear and helpful."

The decision was reached, and now it has arrived in my inbox. I stare at the article—the facts of the case reported, the photograph of the man in prison attire looking angry. I take it all in—how real it all is, my role in it, this man's life, the news. For the DA, it's a victory; he has won the case and he had no doubts about what the decision should be. A man who was found to be a danger to his community has been locked away.

I, however, was not invested in the outcome. I was at the trial just to answer the question of whether or not he meets SVP criteria, and to explain why he does. I was hired to give my expert opinion, to speak about this man's level of dangerousness, as I understood it. And yet, these actions—my testimony, my opinion—cannot be separated from their effect: A man, having served his time for his crimes, has not been set free by a community that believes this will help keep them safe. My testimony was helpful. I did my job well. I'm not sure what I should be feeling about it, if anything.

————————

THE DAY AFTER RECEIVING THAT EMAIL, I get into trouble of my own. As usual, I have my camera with me in the car, and as I park at the prison, I have the thought that I could take some photos in the parking lot before going in for the evaluation. The giant fences and imposing building in the middle of cow pastures speak to me.

But I get too close to the perimeter of the institution. A big no-no. I hear a yell and look up from my camera to see an officer walking out of the reception area and over to where I'm standing. He takes his time to cross the parking lot; I'm the only person standing there among the parked cars, and there's no danger of me going anywhere. Until he speaks, I have no concern about his approach.

As he arrives, he holds up his hand, indicating I should stop. "What are you doing here?" he demands to know. "Who are you? Why are you here?"

"I—I'm here as a psychologist to perform an evaluation," I stammer, suddenly aware he's there to stop me from what I'm doing. "I'm also an artist and I just thought I would take some pictures of this amazing setting." He only half-listens as he calls the sergeant on his walkie-talkie, and repeats some of what I say.

We wait together in silence as now the sergeant purposefully walks over. When he arrives, he says, "Show me the pictures." He looks over my shoulder as I dutifully scroll through them. I flush hot as we look at them, again trying to explain that the photos are for art. My face feels flush and I'm stammering.

He shakes his head. "We can't have those photos out there," he explains patiently, yet firmly. "It would compromise security to have photographs of the perimeter of a prison. People can make plans for escape."

"Oh, y-yes, of course." I flush again. "I didn't think of that. I'm so sorry." I'm beginning to wonder if this may be against a law of some kind—I know I can't take photos inside of the prison, but it never occurred to me that I couldn't take them outside. Is this something they might report to the Department of Mental Health, which holds my contract?

"You're going to have to delete those," he says, and then stands there looking over my shoulder, watching as I delete each one. I feel like a little kid caught breaking the rules. After the last one is deleted, he nods and walks back to reception, leaving me standing there.

I take a deep breath and swallow my embarrassment. But to be honest, more than embarrassed, I'm heartbroken to delete the photos. Some of them were really good. I surprise myself with these thoughts: Instead of wishing I hadn't taken the photos, I wish I hadn't been caught. Moments like this help me understand these men a little more—that impulse to get away with something that I want, instead of following the rules. Maybe we all have a little of that in us.

I compose myself, put away my camera, and I'm soon walking a literal mile through several prison yards on my way to and from an interview—aware, as always, of being a lone woman among hundreds of men. I walk the concrete paths outside through an expanse of blue—the denim of the prison garb and the darker blue uniforms of the correctional officers. Inmates and officers alike are polite; as I walk by, they smile and say, "Hello" and "How are you doing today?" Nevertheless, I'm hyperaware of myself as a woman, the only woman in sight, striding through a sea of testosterone. I'm especially conscious many of them haven't spent much time with—let alone touched—women in days, weeks, months, years, or even decades. Politely I smile in return and say, "Hello" and "Pretty good, thanks." Small smile—not too big. Glances—not prolonged eye contact. Long strides forward. Wondering how I look from the front, side, back. Aware of the many eyes watching me the whole way as I walk. I'm dressed conservatively in casual business attire:

pants, comfortable shoes, a blazer, and button-down shirt. Still, I feel exposed and vulnerable. I'm not frightened, exactly—I've never been approached or had any bad experiences on this walk—just watchful.

There have been many books and articles written about the chemistry between a therapist and a patient. Sexual energy can flow between any two people, so understanding and managing that flow to make sure it doesn't manifest is a matter of course in the field. It would be harmful, unethical, and illegal to act on it.

But surprisingly, chemistry between psychologist and sex offender specifically gets talked about very little. Is this another form of "othering"? In other words, because we see them as "monsters," we don't imagine that the very human experiences of love and/or desire could be true for them like it is for anyone else.

What happens when there's "chemistry" between a therapist and a patient, and the patient happens to be a rapist? This adds another dimension, to be sure. Initially it felt scary to me: What happens when a man who has committed rape feels attraction? Even more scary, what happens when he notices the attraction is mutual? Even when I'm at my most professional, I can't completely hide everything, and some men who rape are charismatic and seductive. Initially I was afraid of these feelings. What would it say about me if I was attracted to "a rapist"? With time I came to understand that rapists are human beings. In addition to having committed a rape, they can also be men who are handsome, intelligent, and even kind and vulnerable. They can be attractive in the ways that many men are.

With time and practice, I've become comfortable discussing all matters sexual, even this. In many ways, it's just like any other feeling—to be observed and understood—albeit with clear and explicit boundaries.

Of course, while we can put clear parameters around actions (no sexual contact), we cannot, in spite of wanting to, put parameters around our experience. In other words, what is it like to sit in a room full of men (sex offenders or not) and talk about desire or arousal? My colleague Martin told me of a study that found that co-facilitators of sex offender groups had sexual relations with each other more frequently than facilitators of other types of group therapy. Does it matter that sexuality and arousal are discussed in a context (sex offending) that is taboo, or even horrible? Arousal can come alive in a room no matter what the topic. Therapists often struggle with shame about this—feeling arousal or sexual energy when talking about arousal with sex offenders—but it is a fundamentally human experience . . . or perhaps speaks to our more animal nature. Either way, denying it can be harmful for the therapist and the therapy, and denies the basic humanity of the patient. It must be acknowledged and dealt with.

And the sea of testosterone I must navigate in the prison? Slightly different, because even though none of the men in the prison yard are overtly expressing arousal, I'm so outnumbered and therefore feel more vulnerable. On alert for my safety, more than anything else. But I've gotten used to the feeling.

There is some reality to my vulnerability; the staff members at the prison are required to wear protective vests to protect themselves against a very real threat of harm. And I've been told about women who have been attacked by prisoners. When I first started the work, my father was not thrilled at the idea of me walking in and out of prisons. He's always been proud of my career and my independence and encouraged my self-confidence, but this seemed a bit too much risk to him.

"I don't like it," he said over the phone, and I could visualize him shaking his head to emphasize his worry. "Find out how risky it is and take precautions." I never did look up the statistics. I know that it is far riskier to be a male prisoner in a male prison than a female psychologist visiting the prison, but I know the risk is there. And I feel it acutely when walking across the yards alone. I'm reminded of it every time an inmate gets searched before being left alone in an interview room with me, only the desk between us.

I have a handheld alarm with me in case I need it, but things can happen quickly. We need to be alone so that I can get him to open up as much as possible, but that entails some risk for me.

Ultimately, all of it is true, and that's what gets hard for people, me included. Sex offenders are people. They're men (and some women) who have feelings and thoughts and dreams and desires and can be genuinely attractive. At the same time, they have, at least once in their lives, crossed a boundary and harmed someone.

———

WHEN I GET HOME FROM THE INTERVIEWS, I decide to peruse the Defense for SVP website—a website specifically for those opposed to the Sexually Violent Predator law and the attorneys who fight these cases. I've heard about it recently and decided I should educate myself. Looking at it today, I find it a bit extreme and hysterical in its perspective regarding civil liberties. One of their prominently featured quotes, attributed to Michael St. Martin, says: "I'm being held prisoner through civil commitment by the State of California, using its Department of Mental Health, for crimes that I might commit in the future by people who are actually committing crimes in the present."

I don't know what present crimes the person is referring to, but being held for crimes that might be committed in the future is certainly dicey. Their premise is this: We are in trouble if we live in a society where we lock people up for what they might do, not for what they have done.

Not only that, but given the fallibility of our legal system, there is no guarantee that they actually have done what they have been convicted of doing. Now and again, innocent people end up incarcerated. It's a valid point and takes me back to the concept of predicting the weather or any human behavior. It simply can't be done with complete accuracy.

The website also quotes Benjamin Franklin: "They that can give up essential liberty to obtain a little temporary safety deserve neither liberty nor safety." A powerful quote indeed. It makes me think about cases like Luke again.

Furthermore, there are some who would argue not only is this an unlawful law, it's an unethical use of the field of psychology. That the knowledge we gain about being human should only be used to support people in positive growth and change—how to learn better, parent better, enjoy relationships, lead more effectively, and live richer, more fulfilling lives. That our knowledge of psychology shouldn't be used to interrogate more effectively or convict people of crimes. As our societal values shift, so do our thoughts about this. The field has issued official apologies in the past. The SVP law could be such a case in the future.

That said, one of the men I evaluated recently has been convicted on three occasions for molesting a total of six young boys. He's continually arrested and incarcerated for his behavior, and then, when freed, molests boys again. Yes, trying to predict future behavior is a dicey prospect; people do change. I wholeheartedly believe that, and the research shows a decline in rates of recidivism in our society at large. And yet the best predictor for future behavior remains past behavior, unless there has been a major change or intervention. As Bonta, Law, and Hanson state in their 1998 findings: "The best predictor of criminal behavior is a history of criminal behavior, and past violence will suggest a probability of future violence."

Typically, prison can actually serve as a type of major intervention to stop a sex offense from reoccurring. Unlike many other crimes, such as drug sales or theft, the majority of sex offenders do not reoffend after prison. Prison doesn't, in most cases, rehabilitate, but for many sex offenders, prison is a scary enough place that they will do anything not to end up back there again. But in some cases, it doesn't seem to do the trick. What then?

What do we do with the man I evaluated who has been convicted three times and still reoffends? Do we just keep releasing him and allowing him access to more little boys, hoping that he won't molest them? When do we decide a person has too little control to stop harming others and lock someone up for what they might do? In *A Million Miles in a Thousand Years,* Donald Miller says, "The great tragedy of our lives seems to be that we are smart enough to ask the questions of meaning but too dumb to really figure it out."

Throughout the criminal justice world, smart people are trying to legislate the answer to this question of keeping us safe, but so far there's no perfect answer. At rare times, I have even testified for the defense, in disagreement with my colleagues who say the person meets the criteria for commitment when I feel they do not. There are very few, if any, cut-and-dried cases.

In truth, my decision is not simply about what someone might do; it's about what they have done—again and again—and what the chances are that they'll keep doing it. It's possible for someone to be falsely accused and convicted once or maybe even twice. It could happen. But multiple times, by multiple victims telling the same story? The threat they pose to future victims gets more believable. The law was created in an attempt to keep us safer, and asks us to decide "yes" or "no"; a decision has to be made if this person has crossed the threshold where their future freedom encroaches too much on the safety of others.

Chapter 12

TABLES AND CHAIRS

U P BEFORE DAWN A FEW WEEKS LATER, I'm off to the California Medical Facility—a prison for those who have committed crimes, but who also have serious mental illness. When I get there, I find myself face-to-face with Alberto, one of the most mentally ill individuals I have ever come across, and I spent two years working with chronically mentally ill people, so that says a lot.

The prison itself is ancient: long, dark concrete hallway, heavy metal doors, rusted iron railings. Once in the office, I read through his file and find a long history of delusions, hallucinations, toileting in his cell, and lashing out at the correctional officers every time they try to control his behavior.

When they bring him out to meet me for the interview, rather than in a private office, we are brought to the lounge of the unit. He's wearing dirty and disheveled prison clothes, is cuffed, and a sheet is laid over the chair before he sits down. His hair is medium length and wild. A correctional officer stands over him and another one sits close by—he has assaulted many and they take no chances by leaving him alone with me. A social worker who speaks Tagalog is there to translate in case he doesn't understand, but it's clear within the first couple of minutes that his lack of understanding is not due to language. I explain who I am and ask if he will speak to me.

"Yes, yes, yes, yes yes." He rocks a bit, repeating the word mostly to himself.

"I'm going to read to you something that will tell you about this interview, okay? It's about the evaluation and your rights." I pull out the information and consent form, watching his face as I do. He looks wildly around, then looks back at me.

"Tables and chairs!" His voice echoes and he laughs.

"Did you understand what I just told you? Can I read this to you?"

"I want my mama. I want my mama. I want my mama." He's rocking again and studying his hands as if seeing them for the first time.

I look to the translator, who says something brief to him in Tagalog, and he laughs and looks down at his hands again. She looks back at me and shrugs. I look at the CO.

"I don't think we're doing this interview today." I slip my paper back in my briefcase.

The CO takes him back to his cell, and while I wait for the officer's return to escort me from the prison, the staff takes advantage of my presence to talk to me about how it's a miracle he can sit for ten minutes now, and what a travesty it is that he's in prison rather than a mental hospital. Because he can't go to the yard with other inmates, he has been locked in his cell most of the time, for years. "That would drive *me* crazy," one of them says.

The staff leaves, but the social worker stays and tells me about her neighbor who exposed himself to some teen girls in the neighborhood. How unsafe her neighborhood feels now. I'm distracted, trying to digest what I've just experienced, and find it hard to focus on what she says and what she wants from me. Most of the time, once people know what I do, they simply want to tell me a story. A story of their own victimization or someone else's. They just seem to want a witness, someone who, they know, will understand it.

The correctional officer returns and brings me back to the office, where I read through more of Alberto's records. Over the years, he has been on different medications and has been described as: suspicious, paranoid, hostile, delusional, disorganized, preoccupied with internal stimuli (makes gestures in the air), selectively mute, labile, volatile, makes nonsensical statements, guarded, noncompliant, assaultive toward staff and others, and defecates on the floor. In the past, he has reported voices telling him to harm others and has believed that he was Bruce Lee or Chuck Norris or made references to the Book of Mormon. He has at least one suicide attempt by hanging and has engaged in head banging and punching the wall and injuring his hands. He often is fitted with a spit mask due to spitting. He mainly carries a diagnosis of schizophrenia. Noted in his history is that he becomes more aggressive and paranoid when officers are present, as well as unfamiliar people. He's currently being forced—by court order—to take medication due to being a danger to others and is gravely disabled. He often requires prompting to maintain his activities of daily living.

When I get home, I can't get Alberto out of my mind. I feel lead in my chest. I bring him up several times to Josh and he nods sympathetically, but doesn't really get why this guy sticks with me. I'm not sure, either. Maybe it's because he reminds me of the disturbed kids that I used to treat, trapped inside an internal world so chaotic and disorganized that it keeps them from living a human life. It's hard to believe, but this man had a life. He emigrated here from the Philippines and had a job; he was married and had a family. They rented a house in Los Angeles and had friends.

But Alberto began to lose touch with reality, molested his daughter, and held his wife hostage. He went to prison and came undone. He became unraveled and unglued. He disengaged with the world around him and engaged with demons, voices, and fears. He came apart, and all the king's horses and all the king's men couldn't put him back together again. And so he has remained in prison. His story is deeply sad and his crimes deeply disturbing. I just can't help but wonder if there isn't some place for him other than this. A life that isn't so hopeless.

———————

A WEEK LATER, I HAD A RARE, opposite experience: I felt uplifted when I left the prison. I met with Tony, a fifty-year-old man who has had a chance to reflect a bit on his life and youth. He appears to have outgrown being a criminal.

Tony is a tall, thin man who meets my gaze and has a straightforward speaking style. We sit across from each other over a table in a small interview room in the prison as I ask him about his life and criminal history.

When I question him about the rules violation write-ups in prison from years ago, he replies, "It's ancient history, lady. I've grown up. I was an idiot when I first came to prison . . . It took me a while to figure out I couldn't win the power thing." He shrugs, hands spread open.

"What went wrong in your life?" Tony seems insightful, and I'm curious about what he'll say.

He pauses, leaning back in his chair and stroking his chin, before he answers with something different than most of the guys I interview: He blames no one. "I haven't been able to answer that question yet. I was a good student, I had opportunities . . . I have often asked myself that over the years." He pauses. "I don't know, but now I focus on what's going right, instead of what went wrong."

I nod, writing down what he has said.

In the pause, he continues. "Honestly, I wish I could apologize to everyone I've wronged for the pain I put them through."

I look up at him, and his expression is dead serious.

"I know I can't do that, but I do try to help young kids head in a different direction than I did. That's not the same, I know, but at least it's something."

This guy almost sounds like a stereotype, but he seems very genuine. Honestly, I'm moved. This guy has come a long way.

Men like Tony are the reason I sometimes miss working clinically with sex offenders; at times it was truly inspiring to be a part of the transformation of someone's thinking, of someone's relationship to the world. To see him go from angry, shut down, defensive, and abusive to softer, more open, in touch with feelings, and wanting to have a better life and to be a better person. To help him understand where he's been and where he's going. This process typically takes years, but I witness a change over this time in how he holds himself, how he treats others in a group or speaks to me. And then eventually his whole life changes—his relationships with people in his life, his attitude toward work, even his relationship with his parole agent or probation officer. Eventually he begins to want to change and finds his own way toward becoming a better person in the world—and his world begins to reflect it back to him.

Several years ago, I facilitated a really tough sex offender therapy group. Most of why it was tough was because of one man in particular—Andrew.

Andrew was angry—angry to be mandated to therapy, angry about the laws for sex offenders, angry at his defense attorney, angry at his life and the way it turned out. The list went on from there. Lucky me, as the empathic person of authority in the room, I was the target of most of his anger. And since everyone else in the group was also newly out of prison, and had their own anger, they were more than happy to chime in.

One day, I was doing my best to avoid confrontation, use humor to create connection, and interest them in the discussion topics. That combination of openness and diversion often works, just as it does with young children, teens, or in the martial arts— deflect conflict and parry with humor and interest. That day, however, I was met with opposition at every turn. To top it off, I was tired. I hadn't gotten a good night's sleep in days; Kye was little then and woke frequently during the night.

Midway through the group, I reached my limit. I just couldn't do it anymore. I buried my face in my hands and surrendered. "I give up," I said to no one, and to everyone, into my hands. The room fell completely silent.

After a few moments, Andrew said, "Dr. Stein, are you okay?" I raised my head and all eyes were on me. I turned my gaze to Andrew. He actually looked concerned.

I couldn't think of a single therapeutic thing to say. "You win," I said, palms open. "All of you. I give up."

There was a pause, and then Andrew burst out laughing. Quickly the rest of the group began laughing with him, including me. It was a turning point for us. I had become human to Andrew in that moment—he could see his impact on me—and the beginning of a relationship formed. It was the beginning of a connection. From then on, the group became an actual therapeutic working group. We all were changed.

This is the part of the work that people don't get when they ask me, "How can you do that kind of work for a living? How can you work with those people?" They imagine the violence, the darkness, the sadness, the pain, and can't believe someone would want to head toward that every day. The darkness is, of course, there. But that's not what draws me to the work. What draws me is that I get to witness the *emergence* from the darkness. I get to see these men become more relational and aware of others, to have remorse and a yearning for something good.

People can change, and it's powerful to be a part of it. Of course, there are those few who cannot—the psychopath or the predator driven by a disorder that is resistant to change while victims are available—as well as those who are not willing to change. But for most, unlike what many believe, the desire is to become something better. Tony, for example, wasn't my client, but he was walking proof that even hardened prisoners can grow. He felt bad about who he had been and what he had done. He wanted to be something different.

All of this makes me think of Luke again. He, too, wanted to be something different. To do something different with his life. I have no doubt I did my job correctly, and the science was good. But science can never fully account for the individual. The decision was the right one legally, but the question of whether or not it was the right one on a human level still haunts me.

Chapter 13

HUMAN

RECENTLY I WAS AT A GATHERING with fellow colleagues who perform SVP evaluations. At the time, I was wrestling with how to score someone on one of our actuarial measures—the question being whether or not there was an "imminent sexual offense." In some cases, this is obvious—if a man is holding down a screaming, struggling woman, while tearing both of their clothing off, but is stopped before raping her, we can score him as having an imminent sexual offense. But in other cases, it's not completely clear-cut—we can guess the person was planning to commit a sexual offense, but not be 100 percent sure. For example, just because someone with pedophilia is spending time with a friend who has children, it doesn't necessarily mean those children will be molested.

I took advantage of the gathering to run the case by my friend and colleague in attendance. While, of course, we had used the measure many times, just to be safe we re-read the instructions for what counts as an "imminent sexual offense": a situation where no sexual offense has occurred, but we can assume it was imminent. The example given in the instructions was of a case wherein a convicted rapist was caught pulling a mattress into a women's bathroom. I'm amazed at the audacity of this act.

"Unbelievable, the gall!" I shake my head.

"At least the guy gets points for trying to make himself comfortable!" My friend's response is quick and wry. We burst out laughing. I know our laughter is completely improper; what the man was planning to do is not at all funny. But, truthfully, in this work, there are times when inappropriate humor is one of the only tools that keeps things from getting too dark.

What could possibly be humorous about performing Sexually Violent Predator Evaluations? Absolutely nothing. But my colleagues, the few who do this work, generally are clever and witty. They provide comic relief in the midst of all that is grim and dark. It helps to have a little levity when much of what we deal with is so heavy.

There's also humor in unexpected places in the work itself. Like parole violation summaries. Typically, they're simply dry and official. Then in one report, I come across a verbatim conversation with a parolee that strikes my funny bone. In the summary, a parole agent pays a parolee a surprise visit and smells alcohol on his breath—a violation of the terms of his parole.

"How much have you been drinking?" the parole agent asks.

"Not enough" is the drunken reply.

It's hard to imagine the parole agent didn't find that a little bit clever before bringing him in.

Moments like this, and the "off-color" remarks my colleagues have made, make me laugh. And when I laugh, I breathe. I remember not everything is so sad or so serious all the time.

Everyone can offer stories about inappropriate humor—something strikes you as funny during the funeral of a loved one; someone makes a joke about castration after hearing about a colleague's painful affair; a friend is wheeled off to surgery and jokes about writing a relative out of his will. Sometimes these moments of humor can be a way to avoid difficult feelings or cover up grief. But just as often, it serves a different purpose. Christine Clifford, cancer survivor and author of *Not Now . . . I'm Having a No Hair Day,* writes that a humorous moment or outlook can help us survive an experience that feels otherwise not survivable. At times I've thought if I don't laugh, surely I'll drown in despair. Humor can also serve as a distancer—to help us feel more removed from the pain of what's being discussed. But as much of a relief as it can be, the distance never lasts for too long.

I go out to lunch with my colleague and friend Steve and, as usual, the conversation at some point turns to the SVP evaluation work we are both doing. I mention I'm currently evaluating a man I'm thinking may be a sexual sadist, since he raped a woman anally and then forced her to perform oral sex, back and forth, repeatedly. This seems horribly degrading to me and makes me want to vomit at the thought of it, and because of my visceral response, I wonder if the act is sadistic.

"I agree, it's pretty repugnant." He nods. "It's just plain gross. But, Sam, there's something you should know about it. That might be important to the case."

"What's that?"

He pauses for a moment and leans over the table, lowering his voice. "It's actually not uncommon in pornography, believe it or not."

"Switching between oral and anal sex like that? Are you kidding me?" I keep my voice low, out of respect for others in the restaurant, but I sit back with narrowed eyes and take a swig of my water.

"I'm not kidding you, unfortunately."

Steve is right; this is important information for me to have. If the offender thinks it's normal sexual behavior—something women do—he wouldn't be thinking that it's sadistic during the rape. I appreciate him telling me.

I suppose it's naïve for someone in my work to be surprised it's so common, but it's hard for me to believe it is. So, when I go home, I ask Josh what he thinks about this, and he concurs—that it's both common and pretty repugnant.

I'm not shocked that I've learned something new in the realm of arousal. If I could make a list of everything I've heard or read about sexuality while doing this work, it would be a book, and most people wouldn't have known most of it. I've come to expect the unexpected and believe that there's more we don't know about arousal than we do.

As I mull all this over, it dawns on me that two men whom I know, love, and respect, my friend Steve and my husband Josh, are aware this is a common practice in pornography. I am relieved to know they find it repugnant, and glad they told me it's common in pornography, so I can evaluate this man properly. But I'd rather not think about how Steve and Josh know about it. It feels a little like I'm invading their privacy to have the information. Worse than that, it feels like work and home are coming dangerously close together—the line between the people who commit sex offenses and those I love feels more blurry. Home is my safe haven from this work, a place where I can go to leave work behind. I don't like the intersecting. I want to shake my head to clear it. In reality, though, it's impossible to hold this work of evaluating sexual arousal and behavior completely separate from my life. Sexuality is human, and so it's everywhere, even at home.

———

I'M REMINDED OF AN EXPERIENCE I had when I was a couple of years into treating people who commit sex offenses. My twin daughters were three at the time, and I was giving them a bath. As usual, I was perched on the toilet seat next to them, ensuring no one drowned, the play didn't get too wild, and most of the water would stay inside the tub.

In some ways, nightly bath time was a chore. It entailed a lot of get-ready and clean-up. But it was also incredibly sweet. Most kids love to play in water; Eva and Rachel were no exception. They were almost too big to both be in one tub, but they had so much fun together I was reluctant to move them on. As they played, my mind drifted between thinking about life and work, then back to sharing their high-spirited glee.

As usual, the bath was full of bubbles and toys and, as is often true for twins, they swiftly moved from solo play into excited collaboration. Their imaginative play began with the toys–there were many adventures to be had as the ships sailed through the mountains of bubbles–then shifted to the bubbles themselves.

"Let's have a party! The bubbles can be our cake!" Rachel's voice rose with excitement.

I was startled briefly from my reverie. "As long as you don't actually eat the cake," I warned, my eyebrows raised as I shot them a pseudo-admonishing look.

"We won't," they said with a smile, their voices in sing-songy unison, and I couldn't help but smile in return. They often did that kind of twin thing–respond with "we" in one voice.

After the pretend cake was "eaten," the bubbles swiftly became other things of their imagination: pretend snow, pretend blankets, and, finally, pretend clothing and hair.

"It's a wig!" Rachel squealed, plopping a generous mass of suds on Eva's head.

Eva burst out laughing and grabbed her own clump. "You have a wig, too!" she shouted, dumping it on Rachel, who laughed with her.

The tub was slippery and in their exuberance, they often fell on top of each other, soapy bubbles flying everywhere. Their deep belly laughs and lack of inhibition were infectious. They were, as many parents describe their children, so sweet, lovely, and delicious.

Eva stuck a handful of bubbles on her chin. "I have a beard!" she shouted, sliding into Rachel as she dolloped bubbles on her sister's face. "And you do, too!"

Water was sloshing over the sides of the tub. It was making a mess, but I couldn't help but crack up with them–their enthusiasm and fun were simply contagious. They swiftly moved from decorating each other's faces to fashioning their bodies with bubble clothing, studiously arranging bubbles all over each other's shoulders, chests, tummies, and backs. My heart was full as I watched them delight in the sensory nature of the experience, completely uninhibited and joyful, simply enjoying the sensations of the bubbles, their hands, and each other's skin, in the free, innocent way children do.

As I was swept up in the enchanting scene before me, my hand suddenly and instinctively went to my mouth and I stood, thinking I might vomit into the toilet. I was horrified to discover all at once that I could understand that the distortion of this experience is how young children can become sexually appealing to an adult. My face was hot, and my jaw clenched with the fierce protectiveness I felt toward them. The thought that someone might use them for their own sexual gratification at the height of such innocence and disinhibition made me want to stand guard over them with a long, sharp knife. And in that instant, I was forced to hold all of it—the revulsion, the fierceness, the disbelief, and the horror—while also having had the experience of understanding. While I may not ever be able to understand the *action* of molesting a child–or even the *desire* to–this experience of my children gave me a window into the feelings of someone who might. Having this insight—about how it's natural, human feelings that get distorted–was disorienting.

I was similarly thrown off balance a few years ago, when I was in the middle of a fight with Josh and furious with him. We were sitting on the living room couch, trying to talk things through and failing miserably—both of us feeling unloved, misunderstood, and angry. I don't even remember what we were fighting about, but whatever it was, it had evolved to the point where we were no longer able to easily resolve it.

Frustrated, he leaned back and put his hands behind his head and looked away as he thought about what he wanted to say next. As he did, his shirt stretched over his chest and his biceps peeked out from under his shirtsleeves. I suddenly wanted to take him.

In a different context, when we might feel loving and close, Josh might welcome his partner's desire to rip his clothes off. However, this wasn't an appropriate situation for such thoughts: He was vulnerable and upset and I was objectifying him. In fact, typically, when people are angry, they feel turned off, not at all sexual. I've felt that way, too, but in this moment, in the midst of anger and intensity, I felt the opposite. I felt red hot inside and a wild mix of things: I wanted to get my power back. I wanted to shake him. I wanted to throw something. I wanted to possess him. I wanted to fuck him.

In that moment, I suddenly understood how things can get conflated—anger, lust, passion, power, and sex can all get intertwined. I kept my mouth shut and it passed quickly as I listened to what he was saying, but the moment had been experienced inside of me. Just like the experience with my daughters, while I would never have a desire to act on such feelings, I could see that they're human ones.

I'm incredibly uncomfortable thinking about all of this. I long for it to be simple and clear, to be just good or bad. I want to feel completely alien from people who would commit terrible acts of sexual abuse; I long for the feeling of *I could* never *understand how anyone could even* think *to do such a thing.* I work with people who do such things, but I don't want to be anything like them; I want them to be "other."

Instead, the more I do this work, the more I'm compelled to hold it all. Deeply humbled, I'm made less superior, less proud, less able to hold myself apart or above other human beings. But while it's tough, I'm also, gratefully, expanded. Where I felt only revulsion or incomprehension, I now have a greater capacity to understand the human experience. It's an experience that, to me, feels spiritual.

Of course, I would never commit a sex offense. That's clear and makes me different from those who do. But if I'm completely honest with myself, I'm forced to see that while I wouldn't take the action, I can understand where the impulses come from. I can see that there's something human at play, in addition to the monstrous. And that impulse exists in me, too. I'm different, but I'm also the same.

Part Four

INTIMATELY CONNECTED

Everything is so intimately connected with every other thing in creation that it is not possible to distinguish completely the existence of one from the other.

—Maharishi Mahesh Yogi

Chapter 14

ACHY BREAKY HEART

A FEW MONTHS LATER, I wake before dawn and drive the three hours to Coalinga State Hospital, the treatment facility for men who are committed under the Sexually Violent Predator Act, and where some men go awaiting their trial.

I'm headed there to perform an evaluation on an individual who has already been committed as an SVP, to see if he still meets the criteria—the law requires these decisions be revisited at regular intervals. "Individuals" is what they call them at the hospital, rather than inmates or even patients. I suppose there's something dignifying about that, but why deny that they're patients locked in a hospital? I'm certain that even when they're called "individuals," they don't forget.

Similarly, the place itself is very unlike what you'd expect from a mental hospital. The building is modern, brand-new, and clean. The central area is designed like a mini town square, complete with storefronts—barber shop, post office, library, modern fitness center. It's a large open space, with floor-to-ceiling windows, lampposts, and large tiles on the floor. There's a giant digital clock with the time, date, and year. Each unit in the hospital is named after a natural place in California—for instance, Moss Beach—the door to each unit painted in a bright, tasteful color.

This makes it weird and almost jarring that the place is filled with men all wearing the same clothes. Rationally, it makes sense, as they're all patients, here, locked in against their will, convicted of multiple sex offenses. They need to all be in regulation clothing and easily identifiable from the staff. But walking through the wide, sunny hallways, past brightly painted doors, through a sea of men dressed in brown, feels more like being inside of a *Star Trek* episode than a hospital. It feels surreal. Of course, conducting the evaluation on someone who lives here brings reality back pretty quickly as he tells me, "I never pay any attention to what day it is here. Or the day of the week. They're all the same." Another good reminder that it's not *Star Trek* is the large, strong, angry man I walk past, pacing the unit, spitting cusswords out of his mouth, unable to calm himself, boiling over as he hisses "Motherfucker" at whoever walks by.

A young, very serious Black man walks down the hallway, with a giant boom box. As he draws closer, I hear the country song "Achy Breaky Heart" playing. He passes a group of white, older men— one has a white beard, one overweight, another has a walker. As he passes, they burst into song, along with the music. Everyone laughs, including the man with the boom box.

While walking through the hallways at the hospital in search of the meeting room, I'm startled when a man exiting the library stammers, "Hi, Dr. . . . Dr. . . . St-Stein." I stop and look over. Usually, I'm in and out of these places without anyone knowing me.

His face is familiar, but it's out of context, so it takes me a minute before it hits me: *It's Luke Miller.* I stand for a moment, wondering what he's doing here, then quickly realize *I* am part of why he's here. I want nothing more than to disappear. The decision was painful enough; facing him here, locked up, feels simply terrible. My stomach is in knots and I want to flee. Instead, I render myself calm and say, "Hi, Luke."

I meet his gaze, smile a little. He smiles shyly and looks down. The silence hangs between us. What else is there to say? I know much about his life; he knows nothing of mine. I wrote an evaluation stating that he meets the SVP criteria and he's here, at a state-run mental hospital, awaiting his trial, where I will likely testify. I'm simply passing through. I turn and continue walking down the hallway.

Chapter 15

MONSTERS

USUALLY, AN INTERVIEW ROOM is available for my evaluations, but today I'm told that the prison is busy with legal business and I only have the typical visitor's option—a meeting through glass. Daniel and I each sit in a tiny, dimly lit concrete cubby on metal stools bolted to the ground, door closed behind each of us. The temperature is neutral, the air stale—there isn't even the slightest indication here that summer is in full swing. The glass is just wide enough for us to see each other and too thick to hear a sound. The result is that the room is unnaturally quiet; we're together, but completely apart. I look at the glass and can see him and a slight reflection of my own face, too.

I pick up the phone, and Daniel does as well. There's a quiet openness about him, in spite of his large size. His frame fills up the glass and I have to look up to make eye contact. He has copper skin and his black hair is pulled back in a ponytail. His size could make him intimidating, but instead he appears gentle, and I have to strain to hear him over the phone, his voice is so soft.

Daniel has a single sex-offense conviction. Nine years ago, when he was homeless and couch-surfing at his brother's home, he came home drunk to find his preteen stepniece asleep on the couch and fondled her. She woke up and fled to her mother. He immediately confessed to the crime and went to prison, where he served five years. Then, while out on parole, his parole officer found snapshots of girls the same age as his stepniece (the victim) on his cell phone. The girls were dressed and smiling, but it was a parole violation for him to have them. He was sent back to prison and I was called out to evaluate him, to see if the photos, even though they aren't pornographic, are an indication of pedophilia and if he's predatory.

I read him the consent form, and when I'm finished, Daniel tells me in a calm and polite voice that he won't be speaking to me. It's his right and I don't blame him; while there's usually a powerful urge for these men to explain and defend themselves—to give their side of the story—most of the time, they don't say anything that will help their case. Occasionally something important is said; sometimes they even make things worse—like James, who played with himself during the interview.

But before Daniel leaves, he ends up spending a few minutes speaking with me anyway, maybe because it's hard to remain completely silent. Perhaps he *wants* to tell his story or perhaps he can tell I'm open to hearing what he has to say. Because I've read him his rights, even though he has stated he won't participate, anything he says to me can be used in the report, so I write down everything he says, even if it's only a few sentences.

Within moments of opening his mouth, Daniel offers his version of events. "That stuff with my niece, it happened a really long time ago," he says, his tone matter-of-fact. "It's been nine years."

"What about the photos?" I ask. Since he's refused to participate in the two-hour interview, I know he won't talk for long, and hearing his explanation is crucial.

"That's not how it seems." He shakes his head slowly, closes his eyes for a deep breath, then opens them again. "Those pictures on my cell phone are my daughters. That's all I have of them." His voice cracks. He pauses to regain composure and continues to speak. "It seems like there are guys who did worse out there, but they treat us all the same. I'm not like those other guys. I made a really bad mistake one night, but I'm not like that. Those are my daughters." He pauses, then looks me calmly in the eyes through the glass and repeats, "Those pictures are all I have."

I listen carefully, nodding, writing down everything he says, trying to show him, as I do in these interviews, that I'm receptive and nonjudgmental—not in agreement, but not in disagreement, encouraging him to speak.

Then suddenly it's over. "I have no more to say," he says quietly as he replaces the phone on the cradle and sits back on the stool. He doesn't say why he stops talking, but I can guess it's about his distrust of this process—how he feels about a legal system, and a world, that has painted him with the same broad brush as every other sex offender. In fact, if he was a man with whiter skin and more financial means, it's unlikely he would be sitting across from me at all. Black men, for example, serve sentences that are nearly 20 percent longer than similarly situated white men, and a 2017 study found that federal judges frequently assign white-collar criminals shorter sentences than the recommended guidelines, which is not the case for other criminals.

I can see he's resolved to remain silent, so I get up, open the door, signal the officer we're done, and leave.

The next day, I open the newspaper and see two stories about sexual offenses. They freely use words such as "predator" and speak of "molesters hidden among us." I read these stories and think of the men I used to work with in therapy; I anticipate the reactions they'll have when they read these same stories—tremendous shame, fear, alienation, and helplessness. Many of these men in intensive treatment have worked hard to understand what caused them to abuse others and how they can prevent it from happening again. They read stories such as these and feel hopeless that anyone will ever see them as the human beings most of them are: people who have feelings and who love others and have dreams of living "normal" lives and contributing to our world.

I think of the men who are found to be sexually violent predators under the SVP law, attend treatment for years, and then are released. These men have, by all measures, been transformed and are ready to rejoin society; yet, their faces, names, addresses, and crimes are published in newspapers upon their release; cities bar them from living there and their lives are threatened. They've worked so hard, and faced so much for their change and redemption, only to be barred from return. I ask myself: *How does the work I do fit in with all of that? Am I making it worse or better, and for whom?*

Statistically, the number of sex offenders who reoffend is small, relative to many other crimes. That number is further reduced with the proper treatment—cognitive behavioral treatment that is research-based and sex-offender specific. In other words, treatment that addresses their thinking and behavior directly, and is designed, based on research, to prevent them from offending again.

In 1999, an analysis of treatment studies of eleven thousand sex offenders indicated that untreated sex offenders reoffend at a rate of approximately 17.6 percent; whereas treated sex offenders were rearrested at a rate of only 7.2 percent within three to five years. In 2002, a meta-analysis (Hanson et al.) examining the effectiveness of sex-offender treatment found that the sex offense recidivism rate was lower for the men in the treatment groups (12 percent) than untreated sex offenders (17 percent). To put those numbers into perspective, the United States Department of Justice tracked the rearrest, reconviction, and reincarceration of former inmates for three years in fifteen states in 1994 and found that robbers were rearrested at a rate of 70.2 percent, burglars at 74 percent, and motor vehicle thieves at 78.8 percent.

The news, television shows, and the movies continue to sell us a very different story. Sex offenders are mostly portrayed as out-of-control sexual deviants who, given a chance, will undoubtedly offend again. They are seen as irredeemable monsters, unfeeling and dangerous, lurking about in dark corners, where they can strike at any moment. Of course, even one of these crimes is terrible for the victim, and we know these crimes are vastly underreported. But the question remains: Does the way we sensationalize these crimes help or harm us? Does it create fewer victims?

OUR AWARENESS OF POLICE and correctional officer misconduct has grown a great deal in the past number of years, as it should. But in the process, we have imbued this population with a sweeping negative reputation as well—just as a sex offender is not always a bad person, a correctional officer is a complex person, too. Some of them, like some police officers, are not people we want in power or in charge of others. But many of them are good people.

Sometimes when I do an interview in a prison, everything goes like clockwork. I'm in, I'm seated with an inmate, complete the interview, and I'm on my way out with my notes. The more usual scenario, however, is not one of clockwork, but rather a waiting game. Waiting around jails and prisons; waiting for copies, for the interview, for some crisis in the prison to be over (otherwise known as "lockdown"). Those days drag on for hours and hours, with nothing to do. Today is one of those days as I sit and stand, walk around, sit, watch the clock tick by minutes, by quarter of hours, and by hours. Sadly, I bid goodbye to my afternoon yoga class.

Sometimes I get lucky and the waiting times can offer me insight, a connection, or something else to learn about the human condition. Today as I wait in the office of one of the correctional officers, a sergeant steps into the office to look for some misplaced paperwork. We chat while he looks, and he ends up telling me the story of how he ended up working at a prison.

"I was raised in the projects." He leans back against the file cabinet. "I had a good mother, but got mixed up in the wrong crowd. Did well enough in high school, but felt pretty lost after I graduated. I started drinking, thought about joining my friends in their gangs, and couldn't see my future."

"It's so hard when we're young to see the future." I encourage him to continue, happy to have the company.

"Yeah. And it was especially hard for me, cuz of where I grew up. But my mother kept getting on my case, telling me to apply for jobs. To get her off my back, I sent out a bunch of applications to all sorts of places, but didn't hear back from any of them. I think, 'Man, even McDonald's won't hire me.' Felt real sorry for myself. Finally I decide, 'Forget this. I'm gonna rob a store.' I get a gun, get drunk, and 'case' the place. I tell myself, 'Unless God steps in, I will rob this store tomorrow night.'"

"You were that ready to rob the store?" I'm honored that he's telling me his personal story, and I'm curious to see how it ends.

"I was that ready." He smiles. "And you know what? The next day—the day I planned to rob the store—a prison calls me in for a job interview."

"No kidding? That's incredible timing."

"It sure was." He laughs. "I ended up spending my life in prison, just by luck on the side that gets to go home every night!"

His story gives me goose bumps. He's proud of the career he has made from it, and rightly so. I can see he's a kind man, and imagine he does his job well. I'm thankful for the turn of events his life had; today I don't mind the wait. Most of all, I'm impressed he doesn't view himself as fundamentally different from the inmates he works with.

He reminds me of another CO I once chatted with, who said that when he was in the military, he was a member of the military police (MP). During his training, he was told that an MP was "someone who was always taking care of stray puppies." He said he was a "tough guy" at the time, in his early twenties.

"Stray puppies"?! What are they talking about? This is about keeping people in line! he thought.

Years later, after the transition from MP to correctional officer, he said, "That guy was right—that job, this job—it's all about taking care of a bunch of stray puppies." He then talked about the rough childhood of so many men he encounters in prison, and how lost they are. He tells me stray puppies may need a firm hand, but they also need kindness and respect.

Having been exposed to the same media and attention to prison abuse and brutality as everyone else, I'm moved by these kinds of interactions—the care shown by these people who work inside prisons every day. The fact that they can see the humanity of the inmates is impressive. I'm not saying the other kind of person doesn't exist; there's no doubt in my mind abuse of power happens. It's just easy to forget this kindness and caring exists, too. Apparently, it's not black and white anywhere. The inmates are not all bad; their keepers aren't, either.

———

I'M SCREENING A BUNCH OF CASES today. Sometimes the Department of Mental Health hires us to sift through the backlog of cases to decide if they would warrant a full SVP evaluation. I sit in my home office looking through the details of one of the files, deciding if this young man qualifies to be evaluated as a sexually violent predator. As I write up my findings, I notice it's his birthday that very day. "Hey," I say to Josh, "it's this guy's birthday today! He's twenty-eight years old."

"So young, and yet he's accomplished so much!" Josh says sarcastically. I try to chuckle and end up just feeling sad. He does seem so young. When the screening is done, I find he's simply a "run-of-the-mill sex offender" rather than a potential sexually violent predator.

"Happy Birthday," I say aloud as I upload the findings to the Department of Mental Health, knowing my conclusions will lead to his release from prison. "I hope you do something better with your life." I mean it as I say it, even if it's just to my computer screen.

———

A MONTH LATER AT MY OWN birthday party, a friend makes a toast to me in admiration. "Here's to the work you do"—he raises his glass of sparkling water and everyone follows suit—"because none of the rest of us could do it."

"Hear, hear!" Everyone clinks glasses and I smile. It's a common sentiment—many people wonder how I could do this work.

"I can't imagine working with people who do those kinds of things," he continues, taking a sip while everyone nods. "I don't think most of us could. It's one of the things that makes me admire you as a person and I'm proud to know you."

A wave of mixed emotions washes over me as he says this. A part of me feels proud that I do work that many people wouldn't even consider. But really, the work I do is only remarkable in the abstract. If I were to say, "I met a man today who raped a few women at knifepoint" or "The other day, I sat for an hour with a man who molested several young boys," most people would react with the same kind of horror and amazement as my friend.

But I don't just meet "a rapist"; I meet a person whose history is long and varied, who has loved and grieved and suffered, who has children and maybe grandchildren, who blushes at a question about masturbation or who laughs at his own joke; a person who has, sometime in their past, done some horrible things. I don't diminish this in any way. It's just that the whole human being isn't only those horrible things.

Of course, horrible things are relative and I'm often amazed to discover where some draw the line versus others. Everyone has their own internal logic, their own value system and way of making sense of things. It may not be one that society has agreed upon, but it's there. The other day, I interviewed a man who, during the interview, admitted to me that in addition to his other crimes he had robbed houses, even though he had never been caught doing it.

"Do you ever leave the house trashed after robbing it?" I ask.

"No!" he replied indignantly. "I wouldn't do that. That's just *mean*—I already took all their stuff!"

I laugh about this later—the concept that robbing someone's house is okay, but trashing it is crossing the line into the realm of "mean." But then I spend some time pondering the concept of ethics involved. Clearly, by robbing someone, he doesn't draw the line of right and wrong (or even mean) where most of society does. Most people would agree robbing someone is not okay and is harmful; to him, it's simply utilitarian. He needs the money; he takes from someone else. But the idea of trashing the house while doing it was adverse to him—it seemed unjust because it didn't serve a purpose. It would just be purely an act of aggression. It would be simply mean.

Maybe he's doing what we, as a society, are struggling to do as we try to balance the reality of prison overload with our fears and need for justice. We have to figure out where the lines are and just how wrong an act or deed is. Then we have to decide if we will punish or rehabilitate, or give someone another chance.

My musing about all this, while worthwhile and even important as an exercise, also feels dangerous to me; I need to maintain clarity about right and wrong to do my work. I remember when I was treating offenders, a colleague confessed to me that in some ways he feels terribly unequipped to do the work.

"It seems like most people easily know in their own mind what's right and what's wrong and where all of the lines are," he admits to me one day. We are sitting together in the office, facing one another on swivel chairs during a break. "Like they have the lines between right and wrong all painted bright white, and lights flash, alarms go off, and God calls down to you when someone crosses over." He pauses for a moment, looking down at his hands. "It isn't like that for me," he continues, looking up at my face. "Most of the time, it seems all confused, and like shades of gray. I listen to a person— how they travel and try to find their way. Things start to make sense to me about their story—then suddenly I can understand how they ended up committing crimes and I can't really condemn them." He pauses again. "I have no problem holding them accountable and telling them it wasn't okay. I just can't condemn them."

I lean over and put my hand on his knee. "This is what makes you especially suited to do this kind of work," I say. "It means you have empathy. And how can someone grow and change when their therapist doesn't feel empathy for them?"

"True, true," he says, nodding. He shrugs a little and goes back to work.

I felt satisfied at the time. The issue he raised was resolved and that was that; the shades of gray give him empathy and I had confidence that ultimately he knew right from wrong. And, of course, he did, just as I do.

But there is this other thing he was talking about that's only gotten worse in me with time: this lack of clarity about things where other people seem so clear. I have never gotten confused about what is right and wrong, or what is a harmful act. But some clear bright line between monster and human, the meaning of certain acts, and where suffering starts and ends—these are issues I have grown to understand less and less as time has gone on.

I don't believe this is true for most people. Most seem to go through life with a certainty about these issues that doesn't change, unless they face challenges to it that they can't back away from. Living in this gray puts me outside of the norm, and, at times, leaves me at a loss as to how to communicate to everyone else.

———

EVEN WHILE I'M BUSY WITH EVALUATIONS, I have held on to a few clients: One afternoon a week, I go into a little rented office and do the rewarding work of helping people transform their lives. I felt it would make a healthy balance for me, and it has.

Today I get a call from a man who says he needs therapy and I ask him why he's calling. He takes a deep breath and tells me his story. While his pain feels unique to him, it's a story I've heard many times before.

"My mother died about a year ago," he starts slowly. "It was a big loss. And then right after that, I lost my job." He pauses to gather his thoughts. "I was really down. I felt really bad about myself. I don't know what started it, but I just started going to these adult websites . . . sex websites. Where you can chat with people. Do you know about these sites?"

"Yes," I say, "yes, I know about them." I can guess where this is headed. "I can imagine it must have been really hard to have both of those losses in a row."

"It really was," he replies, reassured by the compassion he hears over the line. "Look, I've been married for twenty years," he continues. "I've never cheated on my wife. Going to these sites . . . made me feel better for a few minutes. It didn't feel real . . . didn't feel like really cheating. It was all so anonymous. I didn't make any relationships. I would just go on at night and chat and feel good for a little bit. . . . And then even after I got a new job, I just kept going. Like a habit. Kind of like getting a drink after work or something, you know?" He pauses, waiting to see if I'm still with him and his story, to see if I'm in shock, or if I'm judging him.

"Yes," I say again, "yes, I've seen this before, this habit of going to these sites. Even for people who don't think of themselves as people who would do these things."

"It's crazy," he continues, reassured, the words rushing out. "I love my wife. It just didn't seem real. It was just a place I could visit that was exciting. Where I could feel like a man . . . feel sexy or something." He pauses, gathering himself. "Then one day, I was at a conference, staying at a hotel for business. I had a few drinks with colleagues at the bar, then went back to my room and logged onto the site . . . to have a sexy chat."

"Um-hmm," I say, creating a visible nod over the phone, encouraging him to go on.

"I was chatting with several gals at once, ya know? I guess one of them mentions she's sixteen during the chat; then, I guess, later on she says she's fourteen. I just was drinking and chatting with a bunch of them and I just didn't pay any attention." He pauses again. "Later, after I was arrested, I found out she was really an undercover cop. I got convicted of a sex offense."

In California, registration is for life and posted on a website on the internet. Under his name, it will list this offense as "soliciting lewd acts with a minor." A powerful, scary, undefined statement of his crime.

He tells me, "I know I have a lot of issues to work on. In a way, this arrest saved my marriage because everything has come out, and this is a necessary opportunity for me to grow, and my marriage to grow. I need to learn why I engaged in the online chatting and what it was all about for me . . . but I'm *not* attracted to young girls. I never have been. There weren't supposed to be minors on that site—it was an 'adults-only' site. I realize I had bad boundaries that night—I'm not a regular drinker and was not thinking right—and I guess having to register as a sex offender for the rest of my life is a consequence of that. But attraction to minors is not what I need help with."

I take him on as a client and enjoy the work with him. He's accountable and remorseful, and we look at the emotional and psychological factors that led up to his addiction to the sex chat sites and how it escalated to that night. As we wind our way through what got him there, and his life gets healthier, he loses the desire to ever engage in the behavior again. We create a relapse prevention plan, find him an ongoing support group, and ensure that his life has activities in it that support the needs he was craving.

By all accounts, the treatment is a success, but none of that matters to the sex offender registry. Not only will he have to register every year, but when he looks for a place to live, he cannot live within a certain distance of any park, school, or daycare center. He'll walk through the rest of his life knowing that anyone at any time could find him online as a sexual offender.

I put myself in his shoes and find it a horrible reality to imagine. I, too, am a believer in consequences, but I have to say in a case like this, I'm not sure the consequences fit the crime. As an SVP evaluator, do I have a right to say this has gone too far? Even if I don't have that right, I'll say it: This has gone too far. Maybe it's me *especially* who should say it.

What's the difference between a bad person and a good person who does bad things? I ponder this question on a regular basis, and one day I bring it up at the dinner table with my kids. I find, with pleasure, that their answers are pretty good.

"I think a bad person does bad things because they like to do it," Rachel says. Of all the kids, she gets the most angry when people treat others badly. It's an affront to her deepest-held moral convictions. "But good people do bad things for lots of reasons . . . like maybe they're feeling guilty, so they lie or something."

She's hit it pretty close to the mark, I think, and I'm pleased. But I have an ulterior motive here that's bigger than just critical thinking or philosophy: There's something important about talking this over with my kids. If we are always looking to protect ourselves and our children from the crazy, sick, and evil criminal, we will miss most of the crime and abuse that happens. Good people who are afflicted with pedophilia victimize far too many children, for far too many years, because others can't believe that a good man would do such a thing. A man who runs a nonprofit that helps thousands, or pays his bills on time and is honest on his taxes, or volunteers at a homeless shelter, or is a favorite teacher or coach because he's kind and dedicated, can also be afflicted with pedophilia.

Children fall into the trap because they can't imagine a good person would harm them. Denial is far too easy when we view perpetrators in such black-and-white terms as "good" and "evil." I want my kids to understand this so that they will know that someone they like or respect or admire can still cause harm.

But I also bring it up with my kids because of more complex, but almost as important, issues I want them to grapple with, such as redemption, treatment, punishment, and rehabilitation. If we label all offenders with the universal label of "evil," we cease to be able to discern criminals who cannot, or do not want to, stop themselves from continuing to harm others from those who need treatment and can be rehabilitated. This distinction is crucial in a society where prisons are overcrowded far beyond capacity, and sex offenders who may be convicted of minor offenses are forced to live in tents under a freeway rather than receiving treatment and being properly reintegrated into society.

The more we understand what compels these people to behave in ways that destroy their lives and the lives of many around them, the earlier and more effectively we can intervene. The more we can see them as complex, and capable of both good and bad, the more appropriately as a society we can respond. And the more aware my kids will be of what real danger looks like, and how to keep themselves safe.

Chapter 16

CHANGE OF HEART

N THE SPRING, AFTER A YEAR of completing over a hundred Sexually Violent Predator Evaluations, I decide I need to get away. Far away. Not just to go on vacation, but to immerse myself in a reality completely different from my own. My brother, who's lived in India for the past fifteen years, offers Josh and me the opportunity to take the kids to India for several weeks to tour parts of the country with him—Micah knows the country well and speaks the language. I briefly think about the expense and the kids being relatively young for such a trip, but we take him up on it.

Even though we went before the high heat of summer, India was hot. The kind of hot unchanged by fans, which just blow more hot air around. The ancient cities smelled like incense, garbage, food cooking, cow dung, and sweat. Everything swirled around each other: child, adult, motorcycle, family, bicycle, rickshaw, cow, car, monkey, dog. It seemed like total chaos, but there are actually few collisions, leaving me to imagine some sort of order or attention is paid on a level deeper than what I'm accustomed to, like a dance.

The dance of India. After a week of traveling the country, we land in the incredible vortex of a city, Varanasi, and I'm only beginning to understand the seeming contradictions of this place: the absolute silence in the constant noise, the space between people where there seems only a crushing mass, and the incredible beauty and perfection amid the dirt, cow dung, garbage, and chaos. I look over and a cow, standing perfectly still in the middle of the street, looks back. Its quiet dignity reminds me of a shared dignity within all of us.

As I weave my way through the heat, intensity of movement, and constant sounds, I keep Micah (holding Kye's hand) in my vigilant vision, while I (Rachel in hand) occasionally look back to be certain we haven't lost Josh (clutching the hand of Eva). My children's eyes are opened to a life different, a world different, a culture different from their own, and after a while of my brother's gift of total immersion, it becomes part of them—it becomes their own, too. We walk through the streets, bathe in the Ganges, and give offerings at the temples. We are changed, and changed together.

India is home to meditation and yoga, to enlightenment, to ancient and modern culture. India is a world vastly different from my own, but I somehow feel at home here, too. There's resonance. It's more than just my brother's home and the origin of my daily meditation practice; there's something about the people and culture that feels more similar to me than my own people and culture. Perhaps it's the way in which spirituality is fully integrated in who they are, rather than something they do on the side. Also, this trip reminds me of why I feel at times I was made to just wander the earth and take it in. I find myself through getting lost, and I'm grateful for it. It's a deeply powerful trip and I return with a strong and clear feeling that I will not continue to perform SVP evaluations indefinitely. India was, indeed, very far away—not just physically, but spiritually, emotionally, and psychologically as well. A trip like this can really give one a perspective on things.

And so it is that I return from India changed. I'm different and yet more myself than ever before. I know in my bones I was not meant to be an SPV evaluator—not forever. I've grown tired of the work, the repetitive, blunt, and static nature of it. Of the dualistic yes/no answers to cases like Luke's, where there is complexity and nuance. Also, unlike many of my colleagues, I've never been able to enjoy the contentious court testimony.

But most important, I feel it is time for me to finally be more creative—in my writing and my art. Being a forensic psychologist in these high-profile cases means that any aspect of my life can be dragged into court and used against me. So when I write or make art, I'm constantly making sure that I'll still appear professional and impeccable. I cannot reveal the messiness of who I am, which is not really what art is about. I want to make art that's genuine and from my heart. India, with the help of my brother, has helped reconnect me to parts of my lost self.

But I also have to be practical. We can't pay the mortgage without my earnings, and I currently have no other employment or source of income. I'll need to continue this work until I can find an alternative.

Thus, shortly after we return, I'm on my way out to an institution to interview another potential sexually violent predator.

———

Fresh from my trip, this interview doesn't proceed as usual: Typically, my interviews, which cover sixteen pages of questions detailing the inmate's life, are efficient, fast-paced, focused, and take about one and a half to two hours. It's not rushed, there's just a lot of material to cover and a finite period of time—I can take all the time I need, but I don't want to have to come back again, so I've become efficient in my gathering of information. Today the interview lasts for two and a half hours, and still many of my questions go unanswered. William, the man I'm sitting with—large, dark, brooding, and initially guarded—eventually opens up to me and then talks and talks.

About an hour into the interview, I ask him if his parents ever hit him when he was a kid.

"Oh, yeah." He looks at me as if it was a silly question. "Of course. I did something wrong, I got a whuppin'."

"Did that happen often?" I ask casually as I take a few notes. I don't want him to feel there's anything to hide.

"Yeah, pretty often." He pauses and looks down.

"Were you beaten?" I stop writing, gently putting down my pen so I can make eye contact. I can sense there's pain here and I want to be respectful.

"Yeah, it was pretty bad," he says. "They used to whup me naked. It was bad. One time they beat me so bad, I ran out the house. I ran to a neighbor's house to try to get help. I was knocking on their door, asking, 'Please help me.'"

He glances up at me and I nod sympathetically. "That must have been so terrible. So frightening." I feel for that little boy, right through the center of my chest.

"I was so scared." His wet eyes meet mine. "Nobody helped me. Nobody would listen. I was all by myself. I've always been by myself." He angrily wipes at his eyes with the back of his hand. "My parents just drug me back in the house and beat me some more."

"How frightening and traumatic for you."

His pain is thick in the room.

"Yeah," he says, looking down again. "They tell me that's why I started drinking when I was eleven."

"Yes, it very well could be."

The interview continues, and my heart feels open as I sit with him. His story is filled with pain—his own and everyone he touches—the years of drug abuse, the woman he raped while high, family members he left behind.

My recent journey has connected me with myself and the world differently, and rather than just listening with my ears and mind, a space opens up between us and I absorb him through my skin. Not that I've lost my (critical) mind, or my ability to see right from wrong, or even perform the evaluative task I'm to perform. It's more that I'm also experiencing him in his full "personhood," and it feels like maybe that's my purpose, rather than to determine if he meets the legal criteria as a sexually violent predator.

I will, of course, complete an evaluation of William because it's the mission at hand, but my interest in interacting with people in this way is waning. I find myself missing the work I did at the sex offender treatment program; I miss helping these men become different people in the world, helping them work through their pain so they cease causing suffering in others. I want to help people like Luke on their path to creating a new life for themselves. One that includes accountability and prevention.

———————

MEANWHILE, I CONTINUE to see patients in my office. Six months after I return from India, I add a second afternoon. I'm enjoying the work and it feels important. One couple I'm seeing, Diane and Mark, come to see me for a unique kind of couple's work: Several years ago, he molested their young teen daughter. Their marriage was struggling and he had unchecked resentments. He was close to their daughter, and one day tickling turned into touching and a molestation. The daughter told Diane, who reported it to the authorities. Mark was arrested, pled guilty, and served time in jail. Since being released, he has been attending sex offender treatment and living in an apartment separate from his family; he has orders to stay away from his daughter.

Yet, they're still married—amid everything else, they hadn't been able to get around to a divorce. Once the dust settled on their lives, they came to me to talk about what had happened and how to end their marriage. The process with them has been deeply moving, beautiful, and exquisitely painful.

"You know I could never forgive you, right?" Diane asks, meeting Mark's gaze. "Our home was supposed to be the one place our daughter was safe."

"I know," he says, turning bright red and looking down, wiping the corners of his eyes. "I can never forgive me, either."

They both fall silent at this, taking it in.

"I just wish it made me stop loving you completely," she says, beginning to cry. "I wish we could try now, to fix what was broken."

He reaches out a hand and touches her shoulder, then lets his hand drop to his side. She continues to cry and blows her nose into a tissue.

"When you reached out to touch her," I ask, "what were you feeling just then?"

"I love her, too," he says. "I wish I could go back, too."

The room is heavy with sadness. We all pause and allow the moment to create as much healing as it can before moving back to the practical task at hand—facilitating their uncoupling, processing what happened, and filing for divorce.

I feel deeply moved by this work—by the process of holding accountability and humanity all at once. I'm moved by the healing and repair, and by the resolution. I'm craving all these things; the sexually violent predator work offers me none.

A year ago, I was working with Craig, a man who was arrested for having molested a boy on a couple of occasions. He was friends with the boy's mother, and really cared about him. The care turned into touching. When he was arrested, he confessed immediately and served time in jail. He came to see me before his conviction, wrote to me from jail, and continued his therapy after his release.

The work Craig did in therapy was hard, and at times painful. But he was deeply remorseful about what he had done, and determined to do everything he could to prevent it from happening again. He also completed a restorative justice project; because he could not make direct amends to his victim, he had donated money every month to a child abuse prevention organization.

As our work was coming to a close, he confided in me that once his probation was complete, he had plans to move out of the country. We are sitting in my therapy office, reviewing the work he has done and his relapse prevention plan, when he blurts out the news.

"I've already started to get rid of many of my belongings," he says, his gaze traveling to the window. The afternoon sun streams into the office, warming it in concert with the feelings I have about him. I'm proud for him about how hard he has worked and how far he has come.

"Why the move?" I ask, genuinely surprised. He has work he enjoys and friendships, and likes his home.

"It's the lifetime registration as a sex offender," he says, meeting my gaze. "No matter that I've served my time, and completed years of therapy to prevent myself from ever harming anyone else. In this country, there is no path to redemption."

"You feel you can't move forward," I say.

"Exactly," he says. "You of all people know how hard I've worked. And how determined I am to ensure this never happens again." He pauses as his voice rises. "I know I'm not in danger of hurting some kid off the street"—he swallows hard—"so the residency restriction while on probation was humiliating enough. But a lifetime registration as a sex offender? It's just too much. I don't know how to overcome that."

I nod and take in a deep breath, letting it go slowly. I understand his feelings and, frankly, have a hard time imagining what that would even be like.

"There's no lifetime registration for repeat drunk drivers," he says, "or even murderers."

I know he's right. And the worst part is, there isn't a shred of evidence that residency restrictions or a lifetime registration prevents sex offenses from happening. They may help other people feel better, but for no good reason. And the stress it causes for the registrants may, in fact, actually increase the risk of reoffense, rather than help prevent it. When someone is working to create a healthy life to support positive change, stress is never a positive force.

But I don't say any of this to Craig because, ultimately, I don't believe it would be therapeutic.

"Well," I say slowly, "I understand your feelings and your desire to move somewhere and start fresh. Just make sure you have the supports in place that you need and you take your relapse prevention plan with you."

"Oh, God, yes," he says, the words coming out in a rush, "I'll do everything in my power to make sure I never hurt another child as long as I live." He wipes his palms on his thighs and looks into my eyes. "Thank you for everything you've done. It's because of you I'll be able to move forward in a healthy way."

I smile at him. I'm truly moved by this man and his commitment to doing the right thing. "It was my pleasure."

It was.

————

WHEN A CONVICTED SEX OFFENDER is released from prison, he's usually filled with fear, self-loathing, alienation, and a desire to put it all behind him, including any harm he has inflicted on others. He most likely survived a traumatic childhood, has a history of drug or alcohol addiction, and has had to survive the prison environment. This man learned to survive by protecting himself from others; and yet when he's released from prison, he's mandated to attend therapy, where he's asked to open up and form a trusting relationship with a therapist.

As his therapist, I ask this man to talk about what happened, to try to understand his actions, and to build a plan so he will never commit another sex offense. I never stop holding him accountable, but I also ask him to trust me and the others in his treatment group so we can help him disassemble his defenses and change. In the process, he learns about what it means to be human again, to cause pain, to be in pain and heal from that pain, to trust, to distrust, to encounter parts of himself that he dislikes or makes him afraid.

Sitting in therapy every week for years with a man who has molested a child, or raped a woman, exposes me to the terrible pain of his victim. But at the same time, it forces me to get to know this man in a deeply personal way. I learn about his childhood, his fears, his trauma, his passions, his losses, and his loves. And I discover that most of the time—with a few exceptions—underneath the shame, anger, and defensiveness exists a person who longs to grow, learn, change, and be in relationships, just like everyone else.

This is the part of the work that people don't get when they ask,

"How can you stand to do that work?" Which they always do, at some point. "How can you work with those people who have done those things?" they ask, baffled. They imagine the sadness, the darkness, the violence, and the pain, and they can't believe someone would want to head toward that every day.

It's not that I'm drawn to the darkness, although I admit I do find it fascinating. And I don't harbor any secret fantasies of saving the world through reforming people. Really, my drive to do the work is about the deeply moving experience of being a part of someone's change and growth. Of that person experiencing remorse, empathy, and a yearning for something better than the ugliness. A yearning to step outside of the world they've been immersed in. If that kind of change is possible, then certainly most things are.

Of course, I know from experience that there are those who cannot change—the psychopath or the predator driven by a disorder that compels them to victimize others. The important and challenging thing is to know the difference, and to focus my energy on where it's useful—to help someone make a new life that doesn't harm themselves or others and has deep rewards.

This is where the gift goes both ways.

IT'S BEEN MY FANTASY THAT THE GIFT to me goes beyond me—to my partner, kids, or friends—but I'm never sure. I've always tried to be thoughtful about bringing anyone into my work, especially Josh—I don't want to expose him unnecessarily to the horror of what I encounter. It's my chosen profession, after all, not his. And yet, we've talked about the work at times over the years, so he has been exposed. In thinking about it today, I'm aware this can only mean that he understands it in depth, and also that he has become, to a degree, desensitized to it. What does this mean for him? How much has he heard that he would rather not have? That's a piece we haven't really talked about.

I feel a deep need to ask him about it. We are out on a date at a nearby Egyptian restaurant; the kids are at home fending for themselves. The food is good, the music is too loud, and we are laughing and enjoying each other's company.

"Hey," I say, when there's a break in the conversation, "remember when I interrupted you today to get your opinion about that case I'm grappling with?"

He nods and takes a sip of water.

"What's that like for you?" My eyes meet his. "I don't mean the interrupting part"—we both smile—"I mean the part where you hear about the case. I know I talk about my work with you occasionally and I find myself wondering if you sometimes wish you never heard about these cases. You know, the crimes, the victims."

"You mean like Baby Patricia?" he says, smiling.

I laugh, then shake my head and grow somber with the memory. Patricia was one of the worst cases of abuse against a young child I had ever encountered. I left the details out when talking with Josh about the case, but he knew the child was young and he knew how horrified I was when I read about it, as well as the basic outline of the case. I had also shared with Josh how the prosecutor had dramatically referred to the child as "Baby Patricia," instead of simply "Patricia," throughout the court proceedings to pull on the heartstrings of the jury as much as possible—as if they needed it.

My laughter in this moment is about the prosecutor's over-the-top language, but it's also in recognition of just how much Josh knows me and knows my work.

"Yes, like that." I smile softly. "Like knowing about Baby Patricia."

He pauses for a moment and thinks about it. The music is still loud and the restaurant is busy, but the room seems quieter as I wait for his answer.

"Well, it's about my philosophy of life in a way," he answers thoughtfully. "We have two options in terms of managing our life experience: We can try to deny something—not hear it, not see it, not deal with it, ignore it, push it away, or otherwise separate ourselves from it. Or we can learn more about it."

When the music quiets down a bit, he continues to answer. "I wouldn't say I'm fascinated with seeking out all the dark sides of life, like maybe you are"—we smile at each other again—"but because it's a part of your life, I want to know what's happening— what kinds of things you're dealing with and being exposed to. I don't want to push it away; I want to learn more about it. So it's because I want to be close to you, but it's also a fundamental part of how I approach life and the unknown."

When he finishes speaking, I find myself in a long exhale and realize I've been holding my breath. I thought I had asked him purely out of curiosity, but I'm relieved at his answer. I guess some part of me was worried he would say, "Yeah, it has really sucked hearing about stuff. I wish I never heard it."

Certainly, it would be important to know if he felt that way— I would try to be even more protective of him in the future—but I would also feel sad knowing I had exposed him to things he wished he had not been exposed to. I'd be sad, too, at the loss of companion- ship that sharing brings. Honestly, though, I'm not totally surprised at his answer; one of the things that's always attracted me to him is his openness and his desire to learn and grow.

"I'm so glad you feel that way." I take a swig of my water. "I was hoping you would say something like that." Emboldened by the relief and finding myself more curious, I decide to push him a little further. "Do you feel like it's affected you in any way—the exposure to my work?" I'm hoping the effect will have been positive, but I want him to be honest, so I ask as neutrally as I can.

He ponders the question, playing with his water glass, nudging it side to side, wrinkling the tablecloth. I sit patiently, listening to the Egyptian music, nibbling on the food.

Finally he looks up at me and smiles. "I've had a landscape painted for me. I wasn't going to go there on my own, but seeing it up close has been fascinating. I had never thought about the peo- ple behind the crimes and how they got there. Knowing about your work from your point of view and how you do your job . . . I've seen and understood how people end up where they end up. It's given me so much to think about."

I smile back at him: pleased that he feels this way, pleased that he's been fascinated and feels like he's learned something, and pleased that maybe he's even gotten a little bit out of the experience.

"What about any negative impact?" I ask. "This couldn't have been all good." I reach out and touch his hand across the table, playing with his warm fingers.

He pauses again and looks out over the restaurant, then turns back toward me. "Well, there are times I can see the toll the work has taken on you," he replies. "That's been hard. To see the times you seem worn down by the victims, statistics, and sadness."

"Yeah, I could see that." I look into his eyes, then look down. "I could see that." We are quiet then, together, our fingers interlaced.

Yes, it has taken a toll. But maybe the toll has been worth the price.

I look back up at him. "Do you feel like it's changed you?"

He hesitates only for a moment before answering. "It has really changed my ideas about what a sex offender is . . . It's opened my mind. I have a lot more empathy now."

His answer is unexpected and I find myself deeply moved. "I can't possibly think of anything better you could have said."

Years of hearing some of the worst things that people can do to other people has made Josh not cynical, but rather more open. I take this as an indication that I haven't lost my empathy, my perspective that I hold so dear, since he's heard about it all through me.

His answer also makes me think there's something bigger about my life than simply the work I do—a bigger purpose, an unexpected outgrowth. Maybe the ways in which I've been able to open to what it means to be human has potentially had a ripple effect. Maybe my opening to nuance, to shades of gray, to the ordinary nature of "evil," has opened up others, too. This thought makes my chest feel wide open and I close my eyes for a moment and smile.

———

A COUPLE WEEKS LATER, I excitedly show some of my new photographs to Josh—the photos I've taken the past two years while traveling to and from prisons. He seems impressed. *Genuinely? Dutifully? Both? I don't want to know.*

"These are great!" He nods seriously. "Powerful."

I grin like a kid.

We sit on the guest room bed quietly, side by side, looking up at my photos pinned to the corkboard. He breaks the silence by wondering aloud about the interaction between my writing and the photos. "For example, it seems like you have this theme in your photographs that has to do with endlessness. Is that in your writing, too?"

"'Endlessness'?" I ask. Most of the time, I take photos out of instinct and emotion—a gut feeling—rather than an intellectual idea of a theme. So when themes emerge, as they almost always do, it pleases me. Especially if the themes ring emotionally true.

I look at the photos through Josh's eyes and see: endless links of a chain-link fence, endless roads, endless bridges, endless cars, endless power lines. Not the only theme, to be sure, but certainly he's right; there's a lot of endlessness.

I think about endlessness and the work I do. I think about how I've recently completed my two hundredth evaluation. Two hundred high-risk sexual offenders, many with more than one sexual offense, and there's always another offender waiting to be evaluated. I think about the thousands of police reports, of victims' stories. Victims upon victims, each with their own fear, confusion, and pain. The thousands of prisoners I have walked past in yards, the hundreds of files I have sifted through, the next evaluation waiting to be assigned and written. Endless.

"Shit, Josh. I can't keep doing endless."

He takes my hand in his. "No, honey, you can't. Endless is not for you."

Part Five

RESOLUTION

Power is of two kinds. One is obtained by the fear of punishment and the other by acts of love.
Power based on love is a thousand times more effective and permanent than the one derived from fear of punishment.

—Mahatma Gandhi

Chapter 17

NEW PATHWAYS

O F MY OWN VOLITION, SINCE INDIA, I was moving toward an
end to doing these evaluations; now the universe has taken
care of making sure it happened. As has happened every fall these
past several years, California is again in the midst of a budget crisis, and the Department of Mental Health came up with a solution
that made continuing this work untenable for me. They decided they
would no longer renew our contracts, provide equitable distribution
of cases, or promote collegial, learning relationships among evaluators. Instead, we were forced to bid against one another, and now
evaluations simply go to the lowest bidders.

Even after this change, I went ahead and put in a bid for evaluations. I lowered my fee for some of the services, but for the
assessment and court testimony, I was unwilling to budge. This
work, if done well, is unbelievably challenging and complex—to
wade through all the case material with a fine-tooth comb, interview well, weigh someone's risk of reoffense, ponder a diagnosis,
be questioned and challenged in court for hours—I know I would
resent the work terribly if I weren't compensated well for it. I also
know that I couldn't stomach the idea of doing less than my best
work on each case, for each person. It's thankless work, and wears
on the soul, so being compensated helps.

I was not one of the lowest bidders.

Since that time, I've seen few cases (and lately none). Perhaps
the system will do just fine, subsisting on the work of only a few who
are able to do many reports for less money at a fast clip; that will

remain to be seen. Whatever fallout may occur will be years from now when those cases hit the courts. A part of me worries about a drop in quality in the reports and testimony and what that might mean for the gravity of these cases. There's a lot at stake. As for me personally, though, it's no great loss. Maybe I was not quite ready to choose another path, but sometimes paths get chosen for us.

As a stopgap measure to make up for lost income, I've taken a contract with Coalinga State Hospital to evaluate the men who are already indefinitely committed. It's a similar evaluation, but they've already been found to meet the criteria through the courts. The law requires that they're evaluated annually to assess whether or not they continue to meet the criteria for commitment. If they do not, they could have the opportunity to return to court and gain their freedom.

My experience at the hospital has been incredibly mixed. I find most of the staff and doctors there to be smart, caring, ethical, and doing the best job they can to positively impact the patients and help them change. When I speak with some of the men who've chosen to participate in treatment, it's clear that some of them are making changes for the better. One man I interviewed told me that he found himself speaking about things in therapy that he's never spoken of before, and that it was overwhelming to face up to the past, including a traumatic childhood and then a history of raping women. He said it had been too painful to face up to before, but he had made a decision about a year ago that he couldn't live that way anymore: Women are not the enemy. People are not the enemy. He couldn't continue to hurt people.

"There was something inside of me that was still angry and I had to face terrible truths about myself," he told me. "I had to admit that I actually enjoyed some of what I did. The punishment I got should have stopped me, but it didn't.

"I have a lot more to go through . . . I still have some things that need to be taken care of . . . but I'm happy I'm at the point where I'm at and I'm grateful for the help I've gotten so far. I feel I've made some real progress and I'm on the right track . . . I feel there's a good person inside me, he just needs to be reacquainted with the young man that's still in there."

His moving statements speak to a part of the system that's working. However, the hospital is not without major issues. The staff and therapist turnover is extremely high—whether due to the nature of the work, or the remote location of the hospital, is unclear, but it means patients get stuck in parts of the treatment program for years, having to start afresh with a new therapist each time. Also, there doesn't seem to be a clear standard of measurement that would allow people to actually progress through the program—or not. It seems to depend more on the opinion of whatever therapist they happen to get. Those patients who participate in treatment, but don't make progress through the program, get frustrated and disheartened, losing interest and investment in staying with it.

Additionally, as the money available for therapists' salaries gets smaller—also due to the state budget crisis—the standards used for hiring evaluators go down as well. The hospital has begun hiring psychologists who have never performed sex-offender risk assessments, or ever used any of the risk measures to evaluate whether or not these guys still meet criteria. These are individuals facing indefinite commitment and their only gatekeepers have never been properly trained on how to evaluate them.

Finally there's tremendous pressure on the hospital, and therefore on everyone who works there, to keep the patients there. The responsibility for releasing someone who's been committed as a Sexually Violent Predator has tremendous ramifications, especially if they were to commit another crime. Thus, there is a tendency to override a good standard of practice—research-based evaluations—to err on the side of safety and keep them there.

While I can understand this from an emotional, psychological, and political point of view, it seems ultimately unethical to me, and a true violation of the rights of an individual who lives in our society.

One day I'm hit with this breach of ethics in the most overt way:

I conclude in a report on an individual that he no longer meets the criteria for commitment. He's in his late seventies, dying from cancer, and, by all measures, low risk for committing a new offense. Following this submission, I discover that the hospital has submitted a letter with my report to the deciding judge stating that they disagree with the findings. They don't argue any of my conclusions, it's simply to cover their own liability. I find this outrageous. It's politics over human rights.

I continue for some months to perform my job there, to the best of my ethical ability, including finding that there are individuals there who no longer meet the criteria. But I end up feeling largely unsupported, and ultimately lonely. I speak about this to my friend Alison, who says, "But this is why you *should* do the work! You're on the inside and can help make the system a better one."

I understand her reasoning, but the machinery of it all just seems giant, impersonal, and unmovable. Making a change in the system would take someone with far more power than me.

I talk it over with Josh, and he's supportive of my decision to move on. He tells me we'll figure out the finances; my well-being is most important.

Yesterday I spoke with my friend and colleague Martin, who's in a similar position as I am: feeling burned-out, not having gotten a case from the state for months, not sure he even wants to do the work anymore. We used to work, side by side, providing sex offender treatment, and he still runs some groups.

"I have such mixed feelings about it ending," I say into my phone. I'm lying in the guest room so as not to disturb Josh working in our office. I'm looking at the afternoon sun, with my dog, Jessie, keeping me company in the warmth. "This work has been challenging, interesting at times—intense and powerful. And it used to pay well. But there's been a lot of wear and tear on my psyche, and to be honest, I've never felt fully comfortable doing it."

Martin agrees. "Yes, the civil liberty aspects of the work has always made me feel ambivalent about it, especially as new research emerges and things change so rapidly in the field." He pauses. "The science of predicting human behavior is still a dicey prospect. Humans, like everything else in nature, are unpredictable and changeable."

We fall silent as we ponder this and I nod, even though he can't see it. Then he breaks the silence, countering these thoughts with the story of three men in his outpatient treatment group who were released from the SVP treatment program.

"They've clearly done tremendous work on themselves and have truly changed," he says, his voice strong and clear, rising a bit. "They told me that they came to believe it's right for some people (including them) to be committed to a treatment program, that it's likely they would have offended again if they hadn't been committed."

I'm awed that they would state this, and I pause to take it in. I feel the warmth inside my body; to think, we really may have helped with this work—not only preventing victims, but also changing people's lives for the better. Ending this work means I won't know what will happen to the people I've evaluated—but that's all part of the work. I do my job and the system takes care of the rest. Luke Miller will either be released or confined indefinitely. I can only hope that if it's the latter, he'll be one of these patients who completes his treatment on the inside and then is released better for it. Safety for others more ensured.

That evening I sit down with my kids at dinner and bring up the subject of my work. They've always had a vague idea of the work I do, but we haven't talked about a lot of specifics. I've never known how much to expose them to.

Turns out they have lots of questions—about prison, what it looks like, why people go there, and what life there is like. The conversation quickly turns to a contemplation of right and wrong, and what should happen when someone does something *really* wrong. Interestingly—perhaps because they know I've helped offenders change, or perhaps because they know firsthand the unpleasantness of having a time-out—their first empathic thoughts are about the inmates going to prison or the hospital.

"That must be a sad and lonely place to live." Kye's eyes meet mine. I nod.

Rachel agrees. "It must be pretty scary to go there."

"Yeah," I say. "I think it is a sad and lonely place to live, and scary, too."

"Mommy, it must be really hard for you to say, 'You can't get out of prison. You're not ready. You can't go with your family,'" Eva says.

I nod and am quiet for a moment. "Yes," I say, "it is really hard. It's a hard thing to say. I try as much as I can to make sure I really believe it's true."

We sit for a moment and contemplate this, and then I ask, "But what about the victims? What about the kids and grown-ups who've been hurt by these people? And what about if the offenders keep doing it and don't learn from their consequences? Should they go then, even if it's sad, lonely, and scary?"

The kids are quick to grasp this problem and feel protective of the victims and future victims.

Eva nods and says, "That's a good thing you're doing, Mommy, helping them learn to not hurt people anymore."

"I hope so, Eva." I smile.

I do believe I've made society a little safer through this work. But I know I've also helped to strip citizens of their rights. And worse, stripped them of their rights in a system that is far from perfect and grossly uneven in its incarceration of people of color and/or of less means. Years and hundreds of evaluations into the work, I still don't feel a whole lot closer to knowing where this balance lies.

It's clear it's time for me to step out of that world and return to the "other" world of treatment, supervision, and teaching. A few days after that conversation with my kids, I wake up with certainty that today is the day. I get dressed in my armor/uniform, but before I leave, I turn on the computer and type up my letter of resignation, stating that after this week I won't be returning to the work any longer. I hesitate only for a moment before I send.

On the drive to the hospital, I find that in spite of the anxiety of not knowing exactly how I'm going to put food on the table, I'm relieved at the thought of not having to make these yes-or-no life-changing decisions or face the grueling testimony. While I was doing the work, I was able to create intellectual distance between myself and the men I was evaluating—sticking with the forensics. I was also able to create emotional distance for myself from the stories of the victims—the children who had been raped, the women who had been attacked—so that I could do the work to the best of my abilities.

In truth, however, I'm not an emotionally distant person. I'm deeply feeling and empathic, and I could feel the pervasive and acute pain of the perpetrators and the victims. It was taking a toll. It was weighing on me and beginning to weigh me down.

The next day on my commute, I call my dear friend and respected colleague Isabella and tell her about my decision and transition. She responds by telling me she's been contemplating creating an institute that focuses on evaluations and treatment of people who have difficulty controlling their behaviors and are seeking help. She asks if I'd like to join her.

While this would be challenging work as well, it feels more immediately rewarding and will give me much more of a hand in creating a program based on my experience and the research and literature that's current. It will allow me to focus on my writing, training other therapists in working with these challenging populations, and I will even provide some of the treatment myself. Treating patients, training others, and running a business is work that takes a different kind of toll, but one that ultimately feels creative and exciting—and it's no small thing to have a friend working by my side. I will feel supported in this work, but more than that, I can make a direct difference in the lives of others.

The SVP work was important work, and ultimately, I'm proud of it, whatever mixed feelings and questions I've had. When I look back, I can see that my evaluations were fair, and that I was part of a system that was attempting to make our society safer from people who repeatedly harm others, while providing them with the opportunity for help and change. But I think my true gifts lie in operating as an agent of change rather than an objective evaluator and witness. And the constant stream of victims, the intensity of emotion in the perpetrators, and operating within a system that was so broken, all of this finally made it too difficult for me to continue. I need to be a part of something more hopeful and growth oriented—for me and for the people I work with.

I'm leaving this work an expert, but an expert with more questions than answers. In spite of our efforts to forget, lock, or legislate them away, sex offenders, like death row inmates, murderers, gang members, chronic drug abusers and dealers, and perpetrators of hate crimes, continue to exist and overcrowd our prisons. These issues continue to plague us because in spite of us wanting to objectify, vilify, and marginalize those who commit these acts, these issues are fundamentally about people. About human beings who make bad choices with sometimes-terrible consequences, but human beings nonetheless. Our horror and fear alert us to the real danger of living among people who make such choices; but our knowledge and humanity must dictate the decisions we make about what to do about it. It's been deeply humbling for me to discover that I'm on the same continuum of humanity as everyone else. Yes, even sex offenders. But even as this knowledge brings me to my knees, it also opens me up in beautiful and unexpected ways. It creates hope, and provides pathways for potentially new and creative ways to help us all be safer, while preserving the best things about who we are.

SEXUALLY VIOLENT PREDATOR EVALUATION

Luke Miller

THE FOLLOWING IS THE PSYCHOLOGICAL and forensic evaluation of Luke Miller conducted under the Sexually Violent Predator law. I've provided this evaluation for those readers who are curious to see what the evaluations I write about actually look like. Please note that, of course, this evaluation includes the disturbing content of the crimes committed. In spite of there being such content throughout the book, I provide this warning because no matter how many times I'm exposed to details of violent crimes against others (and I have been exposed to much), it never ceases to upset me. While I have, to a degree, become desensitized, I'm human, just like everyone else. It's hard to read about pain inflicted upon others.

There are a few important things to note. The science of evaluating risk of reoffense, just like any other science, changes over time as more research emerges; it changed even in the years as I was evaluating. As I describe in the book, it is incumbent upon those of us doing this work to stay abreast of the most cutting-edge research and statistics and to adjust the method of evaluation accordingly. Even in a year or two, we can learn more about risk assessment, and that knowledge is essential for the best possible accuracy in the evaluations and reports. This is why, if enough time has passed since we conducted our initial evaluation, we are often asked to conduct a more current evaluation. This also means, of course, it has changed in the time since I've written the book as well.

I also feel compelled to mention here, again, that this law was designed to capture only the smallest percentage of individuals who are considered to be a continued threat to society in a very specific way, and offers them treatment rather than a life sentence in prison. I would be horrified to think that my writing would have, in any way, continued to perpetuate a blanket demonization and stereotyping of the incredibly diverse group of people who have committed sexual offenses.

Finally it is crucial to remember that sexual offenses of all kinds are perpetrated by men (and some women) of all ages, races, ethnicities, socioeconomic status, etc.—the demographics cover the widest possible swath. In this case, just as in the rest of the book, all names, races, locations, ages, and identifying information have been changed in order to protect confidentiality. Thus, confidentiality is protected, and stereotyping impossible.

I hope that by providing this sample, readers can most fully understand how psychology and the law intersect to attempt to make society safer, as well as where a case might seem ambiguous or the law might fail. They also give a human face and story to the offender, as well as revealing the complexity of an issue that might otherwise be oversimplified.

WELFARE AND INSTITUTIONS CODE SECTION 6600
SEXUALLY VIOLENT PREDATOR CIVIL COMMITMENT
CLINICAL EVALUATION

I.   IDENTIFYING INFORMATION

Name:	Luke Miller
Date of Birth:	[date, 1974]
CDC Number:	[number]
CII Number:	[number]
Facility:	[County Jail]
EPRD:	[date]
CDD:	unknown
County of Commitment:	[California County]
Interview Date:	[date, 2009]
Outcome:	Positive
DMH Evaluator:	Samantha Stein, Psy.D.
Address:	[address]
Telephone Number:	[phone]
Fax Number:	

Mr. Miller was interviewed face-to-face at [State Prison] by Samantha Stein, Psy.D., on [Date, 2011], in a facility office for approximately one and a half hours with no one else present. Mr. Miller was informed of the nature and purpose of the interview, which was to determine whether he qualifies as a Sexually Violent

Predator (SVP) under the Welfare and Institutions Code (WIC) Section 6600. Issues of confidentiality and mandated reporting were explained to Mr. Miller. The *Notification of Evaluation as a Sexually Violent Predator Form* was read to him, which provides information about the commitment procedure. After answering questions posed by Mr. Miller about the SVP act, he agreed to participate in a clinical interview pursuant to WIC 6600 and signed the notification form accordingly.

At the time of this evaluation of Mr. Miller, he reported to be functioning in his typical manner, and was unaware of anything that would preclude his full participation (e.g., illness, fatigue, etc.).

SOURCES OF INFORMATION:

In preparation for this evaluation, the following sources were reviewed: [list of 43 titled and dated documents including: Referral to DMH, DMH Level II Screen, CDCR Chronological History, CDCR Legal Status Summary, [state prison] Institutional Staff Recommendation Summary, County Superior Court Probation Officer's Reports (POR), County Superior Court Abstract of Judgment and Commitments, County Superior Court Complaints, Police Department Reports, County Superior Court Supplemental Reports, County DA Office case summaries, California DOJ Rap Sheet (CLETS), DECS printout, CDCR 115 Rules Violation Reports, CDCR Interdisciplinary Progress Notes, CDCR Medical History, CDCR Mental Health Screening, CDCR parole activity reports, etc.

EVALUATION PROCEDURES

- Record Review
- Clinical Interview
- Mental Status Examination
- Static—99
- MnSOST—R

II. FINDINGS

A. Has the inmate been convicted of a sexually violent criminal offense against at least one victim? YES

WIC 6600 specifies that an individual must have committed a sexually violent offense against one or more victims in order to potentially qualify as a Sexually Violent Predator in the State of California. According to WIC 6600, the criteria for a "sexually violent offense" is met when an individual is convicted for violating a specified section of the Penal Code and the offense involved force, violence, duress, menace or fear, or the victim was under the age of 14. All of Mr. Miller's sex offenses, police reports, charges, and convictions, will be listed in this Section in an effort to provide historical coherency and contribute to an ultimate determination as to whether he has been convicted of one or more qualifying offenses. Note: sex offense is being defined as any offense that involved sexual misconduct of any sort, whether or not the accompanying charge reflects the sexual nature of the offense.

Sex Offense # 1

[California County], [case number]

Summary

Charges	Disposition	Offender's Age at Time of Offense	Victim Information
PC 459 Burglary PC 220 Assault w/Intent to Commit Rape	- Felony 1st Degree Burglary (Adult Court) - 6 yrs CYA.	17	- Adult female, stranger

Narrative Description

Victim: adult female, [County], [Case No.]

Records indicate Mr. Miller entered the adult female victim's residence through the front door after midnight while she slept on the couch with her baby. He removed her baby from her arms, waking her. He twisted her arm behind her back and placed a hand over her mouth, then pushed her into the bedroom on the bed. She bit his hand, and then screamed. Mr. Miller grabbed her hair and began striking her, threatening to kill her. He slammed her head against the wooden headboard. She kept screaming, causing Mr. Miller to release her and run away.

Sexually Violent Offense

According to WIC 6600, the criteria for a "sexually violent offense" are met when an individual is convicted for violating a specified section of the Penal Code and the offense involved an element of force, violence, duress, menace, or fear. WIC 6600 also indicates that when the victim of the sexual offense is under the age of 14, the offense is considered to be a "sexually violent offense," even if the offender did not use any overt acts of force, violence, duress, menace, or fear to gain the victim's compliance.

The above-described offense does not meet the WIC 6600 definition of a "sexually violent offense" (definition stated above); while the offense might have involved elements of force, violence, duress, menace or fear, Mr. Miller was not convicted of violating a specified section of the Penal Code.

Sex Offense # 2
[California County], [case number]

Summary

Charges	Disposition	Offender's Age at Time of Offense	Victim Information
PC 220 W/667(b)—(i) Assault with Intent to Commit Rape with Prior	- Convicted on 02.24.98 by plea - 4 years prison	25	- Peggy R.: adult female, stranger

Narrative Description

Victim: Gladis Peggy R., stranger adult female, [County], [Case No.]

Gladis Peggy R. was asleep in her bedroom. According to the CDCR Parole Charge Sheet dated [date]:

> She [the victim, Peggy R.] was sleeping and felt someone rubbing her left leg and thigh. She woke and saw a man [Mr. Miller] on top of her. She stated she pushed and flailed her arms at the man. She stated he told her to "shut up" and he tried to pull her shorts down, that he put both hands on her mouth as he tried to keep her quiet. As her and the subject was [sic] struggling he heard her uncle drive up and he ran out of the bedroom and left the house.

According to the [City] Police Department Report, dated [date], the victim identified Mr. Miller at a "showup" and

> appeared visibly upset when she saw Miller and put her hands to her face. She remained upset after the showup.

Sexually Violent Offense

According to WIC 6600, the criteria for a "sexually violent offense" is met when an individual is convicted for violating a specified section of the Penal Code (PC 220 is listed) and the offense involved an element of force, violence, duress, menace, or fear. WIC 6600 also indicates that when the victim of the sexual offense is under the age of 14, the offense is considered to be a "sexually violent offense," even if the offender did not use any overt acts of force, violence, duress, menace, or fear to gain the victim's compliance.

Relative to this crime, it is noted that acts of force, duress, and fear were present. Specifically, Mr. Miller "struggled" with the victim, putting his hands over her mouth to keep her quiet and attempted to pull off her clothing, evidence that force was used. The victim reported she attempted to push Mr. Miller off of her, further evidence of force. The police reported that she was "visibly upset" when she was identifying Mr. Miller later and "remained upset," indicating that she experienced both duress and fear during the commission of the offense.

Sex Offense # 3

[California County], [case number]

Summary

Charges	Disposition	Offender's Age at Time of Offense	Victim Information
PC 459 Attempted Burglary: First Degree	-Felony -Parole Violation - 4 yrs prison, fine, rstn	31	- Adult female, stranger

Narrative Description

Victim: adult female, [County], [Case No.]

Records indicate a Mr. Miller attempted to enter the home of a woman while she slept in bed with her disabled 5-year-old daughter. She reported that he attempted to open the window, looked in the room and "looked right at us." He attempted to open the window, tried to open the door, and then "tried to use his body to open the door." He tested positive for methamphetamine use and had some with him.

Sexually Violent Offense

According to WIC 6600, the criteria for a "sexually violent offense" are met when an individual is convicted for violating a specified section of the Penal Code and the offense involved an element of force, violence, duress, menace, or fear. WIC 6600 also indicates that when the victim of the sexual offense is under the age of 14, the offense is considered to be a "sexually violent offense," even if the offender did not use any overt acts of force, violence, duress, menace, or fear to gain the victim's compliance.

The above-described offense does not meet the WIC 6600 definition of a "sexually violent offense" (definition stated above); while the offense might have involved elements of force, violence, duress, menace or fear, Mr. Miller was not convicted of violating a specified section of the Penal Code.

<u>Summary</u>

The available records for review confirm that Mr. Miller has been arrested and/or charged with multiple sexual offenses. One of these convictions fits within the definition of a "sexually violent offense" with regard to WIC 6600, as it falls within the specified section of the Penal Code and involved force, violence, duress, menace, or fear and/or the victim was under the age of 14. Therefore, in my opinion, Mr. Miller meets the first of the three criteria to be eligible for commitment as a sexually violent predator.

B. Does the inmate have a diagnosed mental disorder that predisposes the person to the commission of criminal sexual acts? YES

According to WIC 6600, the basis for an individual's judicial commitment is a currently diagnosed mental disorder that predisposes the person to engage in sexually violent criminal behavior. A "diagnosed mental disorder" is defined in the statute as a congenital or acquired condition affecting the emotional or volitional capacity that predisposes the person to the commission of criminal sexual acts in a degree constituting the person a menace to the health and safety of others.

While the definition of a "diagnosed mental disorder" is statutorily defined, clinicians utilize the diagnostic categories of the <u>Diagnostic and Statistical Manual of Mental Disorders – Fourth Edition – Text</u>

Revision (DSM-IV-TR) to describe the diagnosed mental disorder. In order to ascertain if Mr. Miller has a diagnosed mental disorder, his psychosocial history will be reviewed.

PSYCHOSOCIAL HISTORY

Unless otherwise indicated, the information in the Psychosocial History section of this report is based primarily on Mr. Miller's self-report during the interview. Collateral sources of data – including the Probation Officer's Report, CLETS, printout, and various CDCR institutional and parole records – will be referenced accordingly.

Family Constellation/Developmental History

Luke Miller is a 35-year-old, Caucasian male who was born and raised in [city], California. His mother is in her early 50's and formerly performed secretarial work; she reportedly works "on and off" currently. His father died four months ago from cirrhosis of the liver while in prison; he was also in his 50's. His parents lived together while Mr. Miller was growing up; when asked about the quality of their relationship he reported that it has been physically abusive—his father abused his mother—and that "they used to party a lot . . . drinking, drugs." When he was 17 years old his father went to prison for a 3rd strike drug offense and was never released. His mother had boyfriends subsequent to his father's incarceration; Mr. Miller stated that none of them were serious relationships. In regards to siblings, he has two younger brothers and one younger sister—the youngest, a brother, is a half-brother.

Mr. Miller was not aware of any complications during his mother's pregnancy or childbirth; however, he reported that his mother drank heavily during her pregnancy. He reported that he progressed typically through normal developmental milestones. In regards to familial substance abuse, Mr. Miller reported that in addition to his parents, his uncle died from cirrhosis of the liver for "drinking too much." One of his brothers has a methamphetamine-related criminal history. He also reported that one brother went to prison for "terrorist threats" against his wife.

During the interview, Mr. Miller reported no mental disorders in his family. The [Institution] Recommended Continuing Care Plan/Discharge Summary [date] states that he did "report a family history of mental illness. His father has been hospitalized for psychiatric reasons in [state]. His mother also has psychiatric problems and is currently taking medication." The report states further that he has "one brother who is mentally ill and has spent time in CYA."

When asked about how he was disciplined as a child, Mr. Miller stated, "We used to get beat up – hit with a belt or extension cord." He reported that his father did not hit them but tried to intervene when his mother was beating them. He then added that his mother was drunk all the time and "Didn't know what she was doing. She tries to make up for it now—I forgive her."

When asked how others might have described him as a child, he stated he was a "playful kid . . . kinda shy. I used to take care of my brothers—when we were hungry and my mother and father were too busy getting drunk I took them to my grandparents house to feed them." He thought his parents would have described him as "quiet." He denied ever having seen a counselor as a child, cheated in class, or run away from home. When asked if he was sent to the principal's office, he affirmed that he was sent there "often" and that the principal even got permission from his parents to spank him on one occasion. He reported that he frequently got into fights with children in the neighborhood and was in 6–7 fights during school. When asked why he got into fights, he explained he thought it was because he was quiet. Mr. Miller acknowledged lying to get away with things as a child; when asked about stealing he replied, "I stole a lot. I used to break into houses—stole from people and sell their stuff to get money. I'm sorry but I did."

When asked if he considered himself a loner, Mr. Miller replied, "No, I don't like to be alone," and described himself as more emotional than cautious, stating that he feels empathy for others. When asked if anyone close to him has ever died, he replied his father, stating that he was "always the savior" and that "when he passed it was a big blow to the faith." When asked about when his criminal history began, Mr. Miller reported that his first contact with the police was when he was 15 years old for truancy.

In regards to his current social contacts, he reported that when he is not in prison he is in contact with his mother, uncles, and friends, and that he is closest to his mother. He reported that he corresponds regularly with his mother, "once in a while" with his uncles, and writes to his sister and brother. When asked how he defines friendship, he replied, "someone who takes care of my needs and I'll take care of theirs." He reported that he has "a few" friends, none of whom have a criminal history; however, all of them use methamphetamines regularly His stated plan is to stay away from them upon his release. He reported that his mother has been sober for 25 years and is his primary support; she sends him money, writes to him, makes purchases for him, and allows him to stay at her home.

Education

Educationally, Mr. Miller reported he attended one elementary school in [city]. He reported that he attended one junior high school but was expelled from the 6th grade for fighting. He then attended continuation school "for juvenile delinquents" but did not graduate and has not received his GED. He reported that he has not taken any technical or vocational courses while incarcerated because he has been attending groups.

When asked if he liked school, Mr. Miller replied that he "liked going to school" and enjoyed "reading—I used to be the first one to go to class." He reported that he attended special education classes from the 6th to the 8th grade; when asked why he replied, "I was just slow—it was hard for me to learn. I didn't have a lot of attention span." He reported that he had a "large group of friends" and that they "used to sniff paint together." When asked how his teachers would have described him, he stated, "My teachers liked me . . . I liked my teachers too." He went on to state that they might have described him as "quiet" and that "other kids victimized me by fighting" because he was quiet.

Employment and Income History

Vocationally, Mr. Miller reported that his longest period of employment was as a mail sorter for one and a half years when he was 16–17 years old. He stated that other than that, he has been employed while he was incarcerated only. He also reported that when he was paroled from [Institution] State Hospital in 2005 he received SSI for five or six months but he did not plan to return to this source of income. He has never served in the Armed Forces.

Relationship History

Mr. Miller reported that he has never had a significant romantic adult relationship. He states that he has only had "onetime things," which he further clarified as one-night stands with "other dope users." He is not currently in a relationship but stated, "I want to try. I don't know how to have a responsible relationship with women."

In regards to children, Mr. Miller reported that he has a daughter who is 18 years old and lives with his mother in [state]. He has not had contact with either of them during his daughter's life; he reported that he has not thus-far provided any support but that his wages will be garnished when he is employed for the child support he owes.

Substance Use History

With reference to substance use, Mr. Miller reported that with the exception of inhaling paint as a teen, he has mainly used methamphetamines. He reported that he began using when he was 15 years old and has used it daily until his most recent incarceration in 2005. He states, "It's a big problem in my life. I know I have to do something or I will end up in jail the rest of my life. I don't like using it alone—only with people." When asked if he thinks of himself as addicted to methamphetamines, he replied, "I'm addicted, yeah."

Mr. Miller reported that he has taken larger amounts of methamphetamines than intended; describing one occasion of being "so overamped" that a friend had to prevent him from leaving the house. He stated that he has tried to cut down but always returned to using after at most two months. He felt his use of methamphetamines has prevented him from forming lasting relationships. He also described methamphetamines as causing him to become paranoid, stating he "thinks things that are not true;" for example, seeing approaching men as ready to steal his car and take his money. He has continued to use in spite of these problems. He denied any other drug use and stated he has drunk alcohol only occasionally in order to come down from the methamphetamines.

A CDCR Parole Outpatient Clinic (POC) Report [date] states that Mr. Miller "reported heavy use of meth. Other drugs include marijuana, acid, and PCP. Parolee reported that he has also abused alcohol." It should also be noted that he was found to have been drinking alcohol when arrested by police after a high-speed chase.

Criminal History

The following section presents Mr. Miller's criminal history, violations of community supervision, and custody release dates in the form of a timeline. The source of data for each event is indicated with a letter in brackets after each event, according to the following key:

A=Sacramento County Probation Officer's Report (POR), 04.14.93

B=CLETS criminal history printout, 09.18.07

C=Sacramento Police Department Report, 01.19.05

D=CDCR Parole Violation Charge Sheet, 09.16.95

E=Sacramento Co Superior Court Abstract of Judgment-Commitment, 07.18.94

F=CDCR Parole Charge Sheet, 05.19.97

G=DCER Parole Violation Dispositions, 07.29.96-03.26.97

H= Sacramento Co Superior Court Abstract of Judgment-Commitment, 02.24.98

Juvenile Record

Date of Event, Arrest, Citation (Age)	Agency	PC and Description	Disposition
[date] (15)	Sacramento SO	459 PC Burglary	[date]: Felony, adjudged Ward, 20 dys JCWP, rest. [A]

Records indicate Mr. Miller was observed by witnesses returning from the back of the victim's home. [A]

[date] (15)	Probation	Prob viol: JCWP failure, FTA	[date]: viol sust (2 cts), resume JCWP [A]
[date] (16)	Probation	Prob viol: JCWP failure, fail attnd schl	[date]: viol sust, finish JCWP, cont. Ward [A]
[date] (16)	Probation	Prob viol: truant 16 dys, FTA	dismissed (new chrgs below) [A]
[date] (16)	Sacramento PD	459 PC Burglary 484(a) Petty Theft	[date]: petty theft sust., cont. Ward, drug cond., rest. [A]

Records indicate Mr. Miller and an accomplice stole two 12-packs of beer from a local convenience store. [A]

[date] (17)'	Sacramento PD	459 PC Burglary	[date]: Felony, rest., Sac Co Boys Ranch [A]

Records indicate Mr. Miller and an accomplice were seen leaving the residence by the owners. Mr. Miller was carrying a TV and VCR. [A]

[date] (17)	Sacramento SO /Probation	871 W&I Escape from SCBR	[date]: Misd., cont. Ward, CYA to 21, rest. [A]

Records indicate Mr. Miller ran away 1 hr and 15 minutes after arriving at SCBR and was taken into custody in his own neighborhood ten days later.

[date] (17)	Sacramento SO	459 PC Burglary 220 PC Assault w/Intent to Commit Rape	[date]: Felony 1st Degree Burglary (Adult Court) 6 yrs CYA. Paroled [date] [A]

Records indicate Mr. Miller entered the adult female victim's residence through the front door after midnight while she slept on the couch with her baby. He removed her baby from her arms, waking her. He twisted her arm behind her back and placed a hand over her mouth, then pushed her into the bedroom on the bed. She bit his hand, and then screamed. Mr. Miller grabbed her hair and began striking her, threatening to kill her. He slammed her head against the wooden headboard. She kept screaming, causing Mr. Miller to release her and run away.

During the interview, Mr. Miller reported that he had entered the home with the intention of stealing the VCR and saw the woman sleeping on the couch. He stated, "I made her put her baby down, took her in the bedroom, cussed her out. She started screaming and I just left. Yeah, I was a scumbag."

Adult Criminal Record

Date of Event, Arrest, Citation (Age)	Agency	PC and Description	Disposition
[date] (20)	[city] PD	496 Receive/etc. Known Stolen Prop	[date]: 60 mos prob [E]

Records indicate Mr. Miller was discovered in possession of a stolen pickup truck with a 13-year-old female where they had parked to "get romantic."

[date] (22)	CASO [city]	10851 (a) Vehicle Theft 2800.2 VC Evade Arrest: Disregard Safety 20002(A{ VC Hit and Run	[date]: Felony (cts 1 & 2), 2 yrs prison [B]
[date] (22)	Probation	Probation Violation: Receive Stolen Prop	[date]: Prob Revok, 2 yrs prison [A]
[date] (23)	CASC [city]	2800.2 VC Evade Police Officer	[date]: Felony, 1 yr 4 mos prison [F]
[date] (24)	Parole	Parole Violation: Dis Saf: Evading, Child Endanger, DUI	SATCU [G]

Records indicate that Mr. Miller was driving at high speeds and running red lights. When officers attempted to pull him over, he was pursued for 15 miles and reached speeds of 90 MPH on the freeway and 60 MPH in residential areas. In the car with him was a 15-year-old "very intoxicated" female. Mr. Miller had been drinking. [D]

During the interview, Mr. Miller stated, "I'm scared of the police. I know I should stay and talk but I run."

| [date] (24) | Parole | Parole Violation: Vandalism, Absconding | IOE RTC [G] |
| [date] (25) | Parole | Parole Violation: Driving w/o License | COP [G] |

[date] (25)	CASO [city]	220 PC Assault to Commit Rape 459 PC Burglary	[date]: Felony (ct 1) 4 yrs prison [H] [date]: 1370 PC CAHO State Hospital/Mentally Incomp [date] Discharged to CDCR [date] CAHO State Hospital /2962 Mentally Disordered Parolee [date] Paroled

This constitutes the qualifying offense in this case. Records indicate Mr. Miller entered the victim's home and attempted to rape her while she was asleep in her bed. [F]

During the interview, Mr. Miller stated, "It sort of happened the same way [as the 1990 offense] kind of—I thought no one was home, saw her on the bed, roughed her up, got scared, and left." After some questioning he acknowledged also trying to rape her.

01.18.05 (33)	Parole	11377(A) HS Possess Cntrl Substance	Parole Violation [B]
[date] (33)	CASC [city]	459 PC Attempted Burglary: First Degree	[date]: Felony, 4 yrs prison, fine, rstn 04.25.05: Parole Violation [B]

Records indicate a Mr. Miller attempted to enter the home of a woman while she slept in bed with her disabled 5-year-old daughter. She reported that he attempted to open the window, looked in the room and "looked right at us." He attempted to open the window, tried to open the door and then "tried to use his body to open the door." He tested positive for methamphetamine use and had some with him. [C]

During the interview, Mr. Miller denied knowing anyone was in the home. He reported that he "thought people were chasing him—I was high on meth. I tried to go in her house—I thought it was empty."

Institutional Record

Mr. Miller received five 115 Rules Violations between [date] and [date] for: Disruptive Behavior (Attempted Battery on Peace Officer), Mutual Combat (X2), Failure to Report and Battery on Inmate. He also received seventeen 128 correctional counseling chronos between [date] and [date], for infractions related to refusal to report or comply.

Records indicate that for most of these Rules Violations, "information provided by clinical staff indicates that based on information from inmate Miller's health care record and brief contact with him, it is the opinion of the clinical staff that inmate Miller's mental disorder **did** contribute to the behavior that led to the Rules Violation Report." Notes by the mental health clinicians state such things as "AH's, racing thoughts," "pt. has poor reality testing, does not understand what occurred. Pt. has significant mental health problems that interfere with judgment," and "highly agitated, confused, highly labile (emotional)." When he was asked how he would explain his disciplinary record, Mr. Miller stated, "People see me as a victim. They push my button so I fight back. I'm quiet—kind of a unique person."

Psychosexual History

Mr. Miller defined his sexual orientation as heterosexual. He stated that when he was 8 or 9 years old his family was friends with another family; the adults treated all of the children "like girlfriend and boyfriend" and that he had intercourse at that age with his "girlfriend." He reported that he first began to think of girls in a romantic way when he was 15 years old and began to use methamphetamines with girls and then have sex with them. Mr. Miller also reported that when he was 8 or 9 years old he was molested by a man from another school on one occasion; the man forced Mr. Miller to orally copulate him.

The SH Recommended Continuing Care Plan/Discharge Summary [date] states that Mr. Miller reported that he was "Sexually abused by an uncle when patient was between ten and 12 years old. He was molested by another adult male when he was between nine and ten years old. The patient reports that this adult male he was victimized by was prosecuted and received jail time."

When asked how he learned about masturbation, he replied, "When I got locked up," and that he masturbates 1–2 times per week; this level has been consistent because he reports he is careful to not masturbate in front of female officers. When asked about fantasies, he reported that all his fantasies are of adult females, and are of "normal, consensual" interactions. During the interview with this examiner, Mr. Miller reported that he was only aroused to sexual contact with adults, and that he had no interest in minors, violent fantasies, or other paraphilic behaviors. When asked to describe healthy sexual expression, he stated, "Two consenting adults."

Mr. Miller's first exposure to pornography was when he was 15 years old. He reported that "it was a normal thing" and that he thought "wow." He stated that his parents forbade it, but that he would watch it on cable TV when they were not home. When asked about subsequent use, he denied any interest; he denied having attended an x-rated theater. When asked about strip shows, he reported that on one occasion he was out with his brother and a friend and they invited him to attend; of the experience, he reported, "It was okay."

Mr. Miller reported that he has never had an ongoing relationship with a woman; he estimated that he has had "maybe 25" one-night stands during his last release from prison. He further estimated that he has had "maybe 100" one-night stands total, but qualified that some of these have been with the same woman twice. He denied any history of sexual dysfunction but states that since he has been incarcerated in state prison he has lost some desire for sex. Mr. Miller denied any interest in paraphilic behaviors; when asked questions related to fetishes, he replied, "No, I've heard about that but it seems outrageous." He denied any sexual interest in children, or having had a sexually transmitted disease, with the exception of "crabs" when he was 25 years old. He reported that he uses condoms and that he hired prostitutes "once or twice." He acknowledged having told a woman he loved her just so she would agree to sex.

In regards to his sexual offending history, Mr. Miller denied any pre-planning or fantasy regarding these offenses. His explanation for the first two offenses was that he entered the homes with the intent to rob them, discovered women sleeping there, and attempted to rape them impulsively. In regards to his last offense, he denied knowing the woman was inside the house and stated that he was simply trying to enter because he was in a paranoid methamphetamine-induced state.

In the SH Recommended Continuing Care Plan/Discharge Summary [date], [Name], M.D. reported that he was referred to SH because "he reported hearing a voice saying 'cut the bitch in the neck' and he consistently reports 'bad thoughts about tying up cellies. Voices tell me the [sic] cut up and rape White women and I've done that in the past and not been caught.' On at least one occasion he has stated that he likes to make people 'stop breathing, enjoy their suffering.'" The report later states that while he was at SH he was "On [date], the patient was placed on one-to-one observation for danger to others. Nursing note [date] states '. . . at approximately 2030 this evening Mr. Miller admitted to having fantasies about a female staff member at the PDR. These feelings involved tying up the female, torturing her, cutting her up, and raping her in the mouth, anus, and vagina.'"

During the interview, Mr. Miller was asked directly about these voices and fantasies. He admitted to those statements, but insisted that he reported this simply out of an effort to pretend to have those problems so that he could stay at ASH rather than be returned to prison at the CDCR. He stated, "I did say that, but I was lying to stay at Atascadero and keep mental health."

When asked if he understands why breaking into homes and raping women in general is illegal, he stated, "It's invading their privacy. It's just wrong. When I do meth I have no regard for peoples' property and safety. I make totally wrong decisions. That's why I need to stop using drugs." When asked about victim impact, he replied, "Putting myself in their shoes . . . scared, hurt, invasion of their privacy . . . they might have felt they were going to die, worthless, afraid of men." Relative to his risk of re-offense, Mr. Miller stated that he did not think he would commit another sexual offense, stating, "I know if I do any small crime I could get 25 to life—3 strikes. I have two already—only one chance out there." When asked about risk factors, he replied, "Drugs." When asked what would prevent him from re-offending, he replied, "Working part-time, joining NA, write a book of poems, EOP groups on the street, classes for creative writing, be busy—not get bored, exercise." He added that he has learned in groups while he has been incarcerated that using drugs "releases endorphins" and that he would need to find other ways to get that endorphin release.

Mental Health History

During the interview with this examiner, Mr. Miller reported that he was hospitalized at SH in 1998 and stated that he was in treatment there for two years and six months as a Mentally

Disordered Offender (MDO); records indicate he was paroled from there in [date]. In contrast with records reviewed, he reported that he is currently taking Zoloft (generally prescribed as an antidepressant), and when asked if he feels he needs his medication, he replied, "I want to continue—to make better decisions." When asked if he has had any outpatient treatment, Mr. Miller stated he attended groups for people with a mental illness for five months and that it was helpful for him; it was initially "scary" to talk in front of others, but eventually he "learned."

In regards to sexual offender treatment, Mr. Miller reported that he attended sex offender treatment groups at SH periodically "when I wanted," and then added, "If I don't use drugs I will always make the right decisions in life." A CDCR Parole Outpatient Clinic (POC) Report [date] states that the plan was that he would be seen "monthly by assigned POC clinician for monitoring and ongoing evaluation."

The above-mentioned POC report further states that Mr. Miller's psychiatric history has included "a variety of mental health diagnoses, including Schizoaffective Disorder, Intermittent Explosive Disorder, Bipolar Disorder, Polysubstance Dependence, ASPD, Narcissism, and Borderline Personality Disorder." It further reports that an MDO status report dated [date] diagnosed him with Posy-substance [sic] Dependence and Personality Disorder NOS (including Antisocial, Narcissistic, and Borderline Features). The author of that report concluded that Mr. Miller did not meet MDO criteria and that his behavior problems were due to a personality disorder and not a severe mental disorder.

The POC states further that a DMH Forensic report (for the purpose of determining the suitability for CONREP), dated [date], diagnosed Mr. Miller with Intermittent Explosive Disorder, Paraphilia NOS (provisional), Amphetamine Abuse, Alcohol Abuse, and Antisocial Personality Disorder. The POC report concludes that Mr. Miller's "diagnosis is not clear at present," and that he was "alert and oriented to person, place, time, and event. Parolee displayed an impressive memory during the interview. Parolee participated actively and effectively in the interview. During the interview, the parolee did not seem to respond to internal stimuli. Parolee reported that prescribed psych medication completely stops A/H he has experienced in the past."

SH Recommended Continuing Care Plan/Discharge Summary [date] states that when he was admitted his speech was "somewhat hesitant" and "intelligence is estimated in the low normal range." It states further that "educational skills are severely limited with word recognition at best in the third-grade range." It was reported that he "easily agrees that he has been episodically paranoid" and that he has been "repetitively advised to rape and this has in fact recurred even at CDC where he has been told to rape a cellie although he would never do so." He was further reported to display "bizarre perseverative clanging" when his memory was tested. At the time of his release, he denied auditory hallucinations or suicidal ideation.

The CDCR Medication Reconciliation ([date] – [date]) lists his current medication Zyprexa, a medication commonly prescribed for delusional disorders or combination mood/delusional disorders. He is noted to be in the EOP level of care. On [date], a CDCR Mental Health Placement Note states that Mr. Miller was referred to a crisis bed due to suicidal ideation. The following note states that Mr. Miller stated, "My ankle hurts. I don't think I'm going to get the proper care and medical tx, so I'm wanting to go to suicide watch." He was noted to be agitated, and have pressured speech.

A CDCR Mental Health Interdisciplinary Progress Note ([date]) notes that during group treatment, Mr. Miller "was content with the group process as long as the process was concerning his concerns. However, as the attention turned away from him he became agitated and requested to be excused from the group." It noted further, "He appears to impression manage and is highly manipulative. Although he reports being slow he has a complex vocabulary and is able to use the words appropriately. He was oriented X3. . . . He is highly defended and actively manipulates his environment to avoid dealing with issues." His diagnosis is noted as Schizoaffective Disorder and Personality Disorder NOS.

On a CDCR Legal Status Summary report ([date]), his parole agent wrote that Mr. Miller "became an extreme danger to society. AOR believes Subject [Mr. Miller] should remain in a locked mental health facility for the duration of his parole. Subject shows no signs of being able to take care of himself. AOR believes subject is a viable threat to public safety, especially for females he comes into contact with."

Medical History

In regards to physical health, Mr. Miller reported he was in good physical health, stating, "I'm fine." He reported that when he was a child he had a head injury that included a loss of consciousness and stitches. He stated that he has no chronic or recurrent health problems or physical handicaps.

Psychopathy

Mr. Miller was administered the Psychopathy Checklist Revised (PCL-R), Second Edition, which consists of a review of relevant collateral information and a focused clinical interview. The purpose of rating an individual on this scale is to determine the person's overall level of psychopathy, a construct similar to Antisocial Personality Disorder but more severe and encompassing. The PCL-R manual describes a psychopath as having a distinct personality pattern involving interpersonal, affective, and behavioral symptoms.

Overall, Mr. Miller received a total score of 28 out of a possible 40 points. This placed him at the 76th percentile compared to other male inmates. Further, the PCL-R is broken down into two factors. The first factor measures a selfish, remorseless, and exploitative use of others. On this factor, Mr. Miller was placed at the 75th percentile. Factor Two measures early delinquent behavior and the chronicity of an unstable and antisocial lifestyle. On this factor, Mr. Miller was placed at the 84th percentile compared to other inmates. Issues of greatest concern for Mr. Miller are related to his need for stimulation, shallow affect, pathological lying, callousness, parasitic lifestyle, poor behavioral controls, promiscuous sexual behavior, impulsivity, lack of long-term goals, and poor compliance with supervision. Such characteristics limit his ability to establish and maintain a stable lifestyle and increase his risk for criminal recidivism, including sexual recidivism.

MENTAL STATUS EXAMINATION

Mr. Miller was oriented to person, place, and situation. He was neatly dressed and adequately groomed. When asked about his current mood, he replied that he was "scared because I'm going home—I have to take responsibility for myself. A lot of people don't have faith in me." As a historian, Mr. Miller has given conflicting impressions and reports over time; it is challenging to believe the accuracy of any of his claims. When asked about how he appears when he is depressed, he replied, "Quiet, emotional. I know how to take care of myself: write in journal, exercise, talk to someone." When asked about suicidal ideation, he reported that he has not thought of or attempted suicide but "when I was a kid—at the hospital—I told them lies to stay there." The ASH Recommended Continuing Care Plan/ Discharge Summary (12.17.99) states that Mr. Miller reported "he attempted to hang himself in 1995 while in custody at California Youth Authority (CYA)."

In terms of his self-regard, he responded to a question about his good qualities by stating, "I like me because a lot of people like me. The staff says I'm a good person. I am a good person even though I'm a criminal." He also listed positive qualities such as "I like helping people, writing, working out, I compliment people, have a good outlook now—better than ever before." When asked to rate himself on a self-esteem scale from 1 (low) to 10 (high), Mr. Miller rated himself as an "8."

When asked about problems related to anger, he stated, "I was diagnosed with an anger problem but I don't have an anger problem," and that he simply has a "problem with guys clowning" by way of explaining his numerous 115 Rule Violations for fighting with other inmates. He denied ever having hit a girlfriend or family member during an argument.

Mr. Miller's speech quality and quantity were within normal limits. Thought content was relevant to the situation, and thinking process was clear and goal-directed. He appears slightly younger than his age, and appeared physically anxious during the interview—he exhibited a slight tremor. He denied any current perceptual disturbance in any sphere; no psychotic symptoms were evident during the interview. When asked about psychotic symptoms, Mr. Miller stated that he only has these experiences while using methamphetamines. He reported that when he is not using methamphetamines, he is constantly anxious, stating, "It's like I'm always applying for a job."

When asked if he knows what the phrase "birds of a feather flock together" meant, he said, "Show me your friends and I'll show you who you are;" he then added, "That was so lame. I feel lame." When asked what the phrase "necessity is the mother of invention" meant, he stated, "I like that saying. It's pretty cool, but I don't know what it means." Mr. Miller's immediate, short-, and long-term memory appeared to be within normal limits. He reported he was unable to calculate 5X13 in his head; he stated he could not perform simpler computations correctly. In spite of this, his verbal fluency suggests at least an average level of intellectual functioning.

His simple social judgment seemed to be intact, as evidenced by his response to the question, "What would you do if you woke up one minute before 8:00 a.m. and remembered that you had an important appointment downtown at 8 o'clock?" to which he replied, "Try to get there as fast as possible . . . call and tell them I'm going to be late." When asked the question, "What would you do if you were stranded in the Denver Airport with only $1.00 in your pocket?" he stated, "Call someone and have them wire me a ticket."

Mr. Miller acknowledged that he has used false IDs or aliases; he denied having sold drugs or used stolen credit cards. When not working, he acknowledges that he has committed burglaries in order to get money. When asked if he has ever left a house trashed while robbing it, he replied that at times he has collected so many items from a house that "it got trashed," then acknowledged that on one occasion he did trash the house but it is not something he would "normally" do.

When asked if he was the type of person who is easily bored, Mr. Miller acknowledged that he is, and that he has done illegal things when he is bored because "it gives me a rush." He then added, "Maybe I can go bungee jumping" instead. When asked if he is a good liar when he has to be, he replied, "I was told I was pretty manipulative sometimes . . . I don't know why I told you that . . . not to get over on anyone or to do anything bad, just slick with my comments." He then added that his "own doctor said I shouldn't be on EOP," stating that he was "too high functioning," citing that he eats well, exercises, has good self-care and attends groups. He concluded by stating, "Because of the fights they think I can't handle myself in the general population."

When asked if he has done things on the spur of the moment he replied that he had, and acknowledged that at times that has gotten him into trouble. When asked if he is more planned or spontaneous, he replied "spontaneous" and added, "I need to become more planned." When asked if he has any regrets about his life, Mr. Miller stated, "Yes: learned how to work when I was a young kid. I don't have skills I need. I wish I had mores skills." He added, "I would take back all my crimes if I could." When asked who he blames for the way his life turned out, he replied, "I just blame myself. It's nobody's fault except mine."

DIAGNOSED MENTAL DISORDER

The results of this evaluation indicate Mr. Miller has the following diagnostic profile:

Axis I	302.9	Paraphilia Not Otherwise Specified (NOS), with Coercive and Sadistic Features
	304.40	Amphetamine Dependence, With Physiological Dependence, Sustained Remission in a Controlled Environment
	305.00	Alcohol Abuse
	298.9	Psychotic Disorder Not Otherwise Specified (NOS)
Axis II	301.7	Antisocial Personality Disorder

***Diagnostic and Statistical Manual of Mental Disorders, Fourth Edition, Text Revision* (DSM-IV-TR):** *The DSM-IV-TR is a categorical classification that divides mental disorders into types based upon criteria sets with defining features. There is no assumption that the categories are discrete entities with absolute boundaries dividing it from other mental disorders, or that all individuals having the same mental disorder are alike in all important ways. Clinicians using the DSM-IV-TR consider that* *individuals sharing a diagnosis are likely to be heterogeneous even with respect to the defining features of the disorder. This allows for greater flexibility and emphasizes the need to capture additional clinical information that goes beyond the diagnosis. The DSM-IV-TR notes that it is important that the criteria not be applied mechanically, and the criteria are to serve as guidelines to be informed by clinical judgment and not meant to be used in a cookbook fashion. The DSM-IV-TR notes that clinical judgment may be exercised to give a certain diagnosis even if the presentation falls just short of meeting the full criteria as long as the symptoms that are present are persistent and severe. The NOS category covers the not infrequent presentations that are at the boundary of specific categorical definitions.*

Explanation of Psychological Diagnosis

- Paraphilia NOS, with Pedophilic and Coercive Features

Regarding the diagnosis of Paraphilia, NOS, it should be noted that the *Diagnostic and Statistical Manual of Mental Disorders, Fourth Edition, Text Revision* (DSM-IV-TR) states that the essential features of a Paraphilia include recurrent, intense sexually arousing fantasies, sexual urges, or behaviors generally involving 1) nonhuman objects, 2) the suffering or humiliation of oneself or one's partners, or 3) children or other non-consenting persons, that occur over a period of at least six months. Furthermore, the behaviors, sexual urges, or fantasies cause clinically significant distress or impairment in social, occupational, or other important areas of functioning.

With reference to Mr. Miller, his behavior can be characterized as repeatedly breaking into homes and attempting to engage in sexual behaviors with non-consenting women. This behavior meets the criteria of 6 months, as over a period of 15 years he was sanctioned on several occasions for these behaviors.

It is noted that these deviant sexual urges were apparently intense as he attempted to rape several women over a period of years in spite of having been arrested and incarcerated for sexual and violent behavior repeatedly, including committing new offenses while on parole. Additionally, in two of the cases he was not dissuaded by the presence of young children. He continued these behaviors, in spite of these repeated arrests and convictions, causing him impairment in social and occupational functioning (including social rebuke), in addition to loss of his freedom (due to incarceration).

Finally, he reported on several occasions while at Atascadero State Hospital (12.17.99) that he had impulses and/or fantasies regarding the torture and rape of women, such that he was placed on one-to-one coverage and "antiandrogen pre-treatment labs were ordered." He reported having "cut up and raped White women . . . in the past and not been caught." At a minimum, this supports the notion of the presence of sadistic fantasies. Thus, he appears to fit the DSM-IV-TR criteria for paraphilia NOS, coercive sadistic features.

• Amphetamine Dependence

Regarding the diagnoses of methamphetamine dependence, it is noted that the DSM-IV-TR describes this condition as a maladaptive pattern of substance use that leads to clinically significant impairment or distress in three or more of the following areas over a period of 12 months: tolerance; withdrawal; it is often taken in larger amounts or over a longer period than was intended; a great deal of time is spent in activities necessary to obtain the substance, use the substance, or recover from its effects; important social, occupational, or recreational activities are given up or reduced because of substance use, and/or the substance use; is continued despite knowledge of having a persistent or recurrent physical or psychological problem that is likely to have been caused or exacerbated by the substance.

With reference to Mr. Miller, he reported that he began using methamphetamines when he was 15 years old and has used it daily until his most recent incarceration in 2005; he self-reported that he feels he is "addicted." Mr. Miller reported that he has taken larger amounts of methamphetamines than intended; describing one occasion of being "so over-amped" that a friend had to prevent him from leaving the house. He stated that he has tried to cut down but always returned to using after at most two months. He felt his use of methamphetamines has prevented him from forming lasting relationships (social loss). He also described methamphetamines as causing him to become paranoid, stating he "thinks things that are not true;" for example, seeing approaching men as ready to steal his car and take his money (exacerbation of psychological problem). He has continued to use in spite of these problems. Finally, he tested positive for use of methamphetamines when arrested for much of his criminal behavior (social, occupational, recreational loss).

- Alcohol Abuse

Regarding the diagnosis of alcohol abuse, it is noted that the DSM-IV-TR describes substance abuse as a maladaptive pattern of substance use that leads to clinically significant impairment or distress within a 12-month period as manifested by one or more of the following: failure to fulfill a major role, use when it is physically hazardous, substance-related legal problems, and continued use despite recurrent social or interpersonal problems caused by the substance.

With reference to Mr. Miller he was involved in a high-speed chase from police while intoxicated, which can be seen as physically hazardous and causing legal problems. In spite of this, he has continued to use it.

- Antisocial Personality Disorder

Regarding the diagnosis of Antisocial Personality Disorder, it is noted that the DSM-IV-TR describes Antisocial Personality Disorder as a pervasive pattern of disregard for and violation of the rights of others occurring since age 15 years. Additionally, there must be evidence of Conduct Disorder with onset before age 15 years.

With reference to Mr. Miller, his criminal record indicates a failure to conform to social norms with respect to lawful behavior. He has repeatedly engaged in physical assaults and aggressiveness towards others. He has demonstrated consistent lack of remorse regarding most of his harmful behavior towards others. His self-report during the interview was grossly inconsistent with the records, indicating that he is deceitful repeatedly and with comfort. Additionally, there is evidence of symptoms of conduct disorder before age 15 years, such as lying, stealing, fighting, early sexual behavior, and early drug use. Further, he was made a ward of the court at the age of 15 and had four significant arrests before the age of 18. Therefore, he clearly meets the criteria for Antisocial Personality Disorder; overall, it appears his personality disorder is currently in the moderate to severe range.

In regards to the diagnosis of Psychotic Disorder, NOS, it seems clear that Mr. Miller has manifested psychotic and mood disorder symptoms over many years and has been diagnosed with multiple different disorders, such as Schizoaffective Disorder, Bipolar Disorder with Psychotic Features, etc. There was not enough information during the course of this evaluation to determine a clear diagnostic picture that would determine which psychotic and/or mood disorder diagnosis most accurately fits Mr. Miller.

Finally, Mr. Miller was also considered for other diagnoses he has carried over a period of years, such as Attention Deficit Disorder, Borderline Intellectual Functioning/Mild Mental Retardation, and Intermittent Explosive Disorder/Impulse Disorder NOS. However, there was not enough information to support such diagnoses for the purposes of this evaluation.

<u>Conclusion Regarding Criterion B</u>

Relative to the WIC 6600 definition of a mental disorder, it is noted that the statute defines a mental disorder in the following way:

> Diagnosed Mental Disorder includes a congenital or acquired condition affecting the emotional or volitional capacity that predisposes the person to the commission of criminal sexual acts in a degree constituting the person a menace to the health and safety of others.

In the opinion of this evaluator, Mr. Miller suffers from such a condition. Specifically, Mr. Miller's volitional capacity is affected by this condition in that he attempted to rape multiple women over the course of years, and despite the fact that to do so not only violates laws and social norms but results in societal rebuke and loss of freedom. Furthermore, Mr. Miller's condition affects his emotional capacity in that despite his victim's distress and the presence of young children, he continued to attempt to rape them, demonstrating insensitivity and callousness. Finally, he repeatedly admitted to impulses and/ or fantasies regarding the torture and rape of women such that he was an imminent danger to women even while hospitalized at ASH. Having this type of sexual attraction predisposes him to the commission of criminal sexual acts in a degree constituting him a menace to the health and safety of others. Therefore, in my opinion, Mr. Miller also meets the second of the three criteria to be eligible for commitment as a sexually violent predator.

C. Is the inmate likely to engage in sexually violent predatory criminal behavior as a result of his or her diagnosed mental disorder without appropriate treatment and custody? YES

In order to assess Mr. Miller's risk of sexual re-offense he was scored on three actuarial instruments that provide general base rates of sexual re-offense for offenders similar to Mr. Miller. These instruments include the Static-99, STABLE-2000, and the Minnesota Sex Offender Screening Tool-Revised (MnSOST-R). All three instruments have been subject to multiple validation studies that have established their usefulness in predicting sexual re-offense. Multiple actuarial instruments are used for a number of reasons. Given that it cannot be known in advance which scale will work best for a particular sample, having consistent results on many measures gives increased confidence in the results. Also trivial or seemingly arbitrary scoring decisions should have less influence if there are several different measures.

RISK ASSESSMENT

First, in order to establish a baseline level of risk that Mr. Miller will commit another sexually violent offense, he was scored on the Static-99 which is an actuarial measure of risk for sexual offense recidivism. This instrument has been shown to be a moderate predictor of sexual re-offense, which was defined on this instrument of being <u>convicted</u> of a new sexual offense.

The Index Offense (i.e., most recent officially recorded sexual offense) that was used to score the Static-99 in Mr. Miller's case is the conviction in [date] for Assault to Commit Rape.

Mr. Miller received a total score of **5** on the Static-99[1] so that he most closely resembles the group of sexual offenders who are described at a <u>Medium-High</u> risk for being charged or convicted of another sexual offense.

The scores for the specific factors are listed in the following table:

STATIC-99 SCORE SUMMARY

Risk Factor	Scores
	Yes = 1, No = 2
1 Under age 25 at release?	0
2 Single (no two-year relationship)?	1
3 Index non-sexual violence, any conviction?	0
4 Prior non-sexual violence, any convictions?	0
5 Prior sex offenses?	1
6 Prior sentencing dates (excluding index)?	1
7 Convictions for non-contact sex offenses?	0
8 Any unrelated victims?	1
9 Any stranger victims?	1
10 Any male victims?	0
TOTAL SCORE =	5

There have been a large number of studies examining the sexual recidivism rates associated with Static-99 scores. Harris, Helmus, Hanson & Thornton (2008)[2] summarized the results of 18 samples of sexual offenders (N=6,406) drawn from different countries including Canada, the United States, New Zealand,

1. Hanson, R.K., & Thornton, D. (2000). Static-99: Improving risk assessments for sex offenders: A comparison of three actuarial scales . *Law and Human Behavior*. 24. 119–136.

2. Harris, A. J. R., Helmus, L., Hanson, R. K., & Thornton, D. (2008, October). *Are new norms needed for Static-99?* Paper presented at the 27th Annual Research and Treatment Conference of the Association for the Treatment of Sexual Abusers, Atlanta. GA.

the United Kingdom, and Western Europe. In the studies used to develop these norms, recidivism was defined as charges in about half of the cases and as convictions in the other half.[3]

These recent studies found that the ability of Static-99 to rank relative risk is reasonably consistent across samples and settings, but the observed recidivism rates vary across samples. Specifically, the average recidivism rates associated with each score are lower in contemporary samples (1990s and more recent) than in the original developmental samples, who were primarily released during the 1970s and 1980s. Consequently, the developers of Static-99 recommend that the original norms be replaced by new norms based on samples that are more recent, more representative, and larger than the original samples.

Research has also found that there is meaningful variation in the recidivism rates based on factors not measured by Static-99. Samples that were pre-selected to be high risk (5 samples) show the highest recidivism rates, and the routine samples from the Correctional Service of Canada (CSC; 5 samples) show recidivism[4] rates substantially lower than the original developmental samples. Consequently, in order to evaluate the recidivism risk of Mr. Miller, we need to consider the extent to which he more closely resembles the typical member of the high-risk samples or the typical member of the CSC samples.

---

3. Convictions provide a conservative estimate of sexual offending as research has shown that most sexual crimes do not result in charges or convictions, and when protected from prosecution, sexual offenders report they have committed more sexual crimes than they have been caught for. Another important consideration is that risk for re-offense increases as the opportunity time to re-offend increases. Thus, although the new Static-99 norms provide rates for a maximum of a 10-year period, cumulative risk continues to increase after 10 years. This is important because WIC 6600 requires that lifetime risk of re-offense, as indicated by additional criminal sexual behavior, rather than additional arrests, be determined.

4. Bonta, J., & Andrews, D. A. (2007). Risk-need-responsivity model for offender assessment and rehabilitation. (User Report 2007-05). Public Safety and Emergency Preparedness, Ottawa, Canada.

The differences between the high-risk and CSC samples are not fully known; nevertheless, the following features are worth considering. The typical member of the CSC samples would have graduated from both specialized sexual offender treatment programs as well as programs addressing other areas of skill deficits needs. Since the 1990s, CSC treatment programs have been based on principles that are known to be effective in reducing criminal recidivism. As well, the typical member of the CSC samples would have been supported through a gradual re-integration into the community by parole supervision and human service programming.

In contrast, members of the high-risk sample included offenders who resisted or failed to complete treatment, and those whose antisocial behavior during incarceration was sufficiently problematic to compel the conclusion that their criminal propensities were still active. As well, the high-risk groups included offenders who had been judged by the court to have a risk that was sufficiently high to warrant exceptional measures (preventive detention, treatment orders, refusal of statutory release).

Recidivism norms for both the CSC and the high-risk group are now available in the 2008 update of recidivism rates. These norms now apply to scores from 0 to 10+. The new risk estimates are determined by logistic regression. This is because logistic regression takes into account the recidivism rate associated with a single score in the context of the overall relationship between the Static-99 and recidivism. This reduces the impact of fluke variations in the observed recidivism rates that are due to fewer subjects within a given subgroup. The logistic regression estimates of recidivism are "bounded" by the lower risk estimates found in the CSC samples and the higher rates found in the high-risk samples for each cutoff score on the Static-99.

It should be noted that the Static-99 underestimates the probability that he will <u>commit</u> a new sexual offense. In other words, it is well known that many sexual offenses go unreported and undetected. Therefore, the probability that an offender will commit a new sexual offense is necessarily higher than the probability that he will be detected, arrested, prosecuted and convicted of committing a new sexual offense.

It should also be noted that there is ample evidence that Mr. Miller's most recent conviction and parole violation for attempted burglary was, in fact, another attempt to commit a new sexual offense; the woman witnessed Mr. Miller viewing her in her bed and continuing to try to gain access to her home. However, this incident was not included in the scoring of the Static-99.

Mr. Miller scored a **5** on the Static-99. The range of risk of re-offense for this score on the Static-99. Within the group scoring at this level or greater, 33% were convicted for a new sexual offense within five years of their release from custody, 38% within ten years, and 40% were convicted for a new sexual offense within fifteen years of release.

Mr. Miller has features most similar to the high-risk samples rather than the low-risk (CSC) samples. Mr. Miller had multiple 115 Rules Violations while in prison, indicating his behavior while incarcerated was antisocial. Additionally, it is unknown the extent to which he participated in sexual offender treatment; his last offense was subsequent to that treatment. Consequently, it seems Mr. Miller's recidivism risk at this time should be closer to the rates for the high-risk samples than the routine CSC samples.

While the Static-99 provides a reasonable baseline for sexual re-offense potential, it does not include a complete evaluation of risk factors known to be associated with sexual offense recidivism. The following empirically derived static and dynamic risk factors are not accounted for by the use of the Static-99 alone and were therefore also considered in conjunction with the Static-99. Protective factors were also considered.

The Minnesota Sex Offender Screening Tool-Revised (MnSOST-R)

The Minnesota Sex Offender Screening Tool-Revised (MnSOST-R) has also been shown to be a moderate predictor of sexual re-offense and it provides the likelihood of re-arrest for a sexual offense for a period of six years post-incarceration. The instrument was developed on offenders who were convicted of either rape or extrafamilial sex offense. On the MnSOST-R, Mr. Miller received a score of **8**. This score falls in the High range of sexual re-offense (defined as a score of 8 and above) and for the MnSOST-R aggregate sample, on average, 57% of offenders in the high range sexually re-offended. This lends further weight to the assertion his risk is higher than the Static-99 estimated level of sexual re-offense.

For the MnSOST-R, new unpublished Minnesota data indicates old probabilities of sexual re-arrest are inflated. The existing probabilities are recorded below; however, it should be noted that in contemporary samples, those who have community supervision the rates are lower while on community supervision. Those subjects with lower recidivism rates were subject to five years of community supervision.

The following table provides a comparison of each risk instrument utilized:

Instrument	Score	Risk Category	5-Yr. Est.	6-Yr. Est.	10-Yr. Est.
Static-99R	5	Medium-High	33%		38%
MnSOST-R	8	High		57%	

Other Static Empirical Risk Factors

A static risk factor for sexual re-offense refers to a variable associated with sexual re-offense recidivism that usually does not change over time. The following are some static risk factors that are not scored in entirety on the actuarial instruments, but have been shown to be significantly related, through research, to sexual recidivism.

- Sexual Deviance Variables
  - Sex offenses against two or more children under the age of 12 with at least one unrelated child victim
  - Sex offenses as a juvenile (under age 18) and as an adult

Relative to Mr. Miller, he was not convicted of molesting any children under the age of 12; however, he committed sexual offenses while a juvenile and as an adult. This cluster, therefore, supports the assertion his risk is higher than the Static-99 estimated risk level of sexual re-offense.

- Treatment
  - Dropping out of/ejected from the most recent attempt at sex offender-specific treatment

Research has shown that those who begin, but drop out of or are ejected from, sexual offender-specific treatment are more likely to sexually re-offend than either those who never began treatment or those who begin and complete treatment. Relative to Mr. Miller, he reported that he participated inconsistently in a sexual offender treatment program; there is not enough information available to determine if this would qualify as dropping out of treatment. It is unknown, then, how this factor might affect the Static-99 estimate.

- General Criminality/Lifestyle Instability
  - Childhood maladjustment as defined by two or more of the following instances separated by more than 12 months—History of grade failure, psychiatric treatment, group home placement, or running away from home
  - Criteria for conduct disorder met
  - Psychopathy [(Hare Psychopathy Checklist-

Revised (PCL-R) of 30 or above)]

– Violation of conditional release or a new offense while on community supervision

– Frequently unemployed as defined by the inmate being employed less than 50 percent of the last 12 months prior to incarceration

In regards to Mr. Miller, he was sanctioned on multiple occasions as a juvenile and was placed in a group home. He also acknowledged regularly fighting other children and shoplifting. There is evidence to suggest childhood maladjustment and a diagnosis of conduct disorder.

Mr. Miller has repeatedly violated his conditional release, including committing new offenses while on community supervision. He was not employed for more than 50 percent of the last 12 months prior to incarceration.

Taking all of the above items into consideration, overall this cluster supports the assertion his risk is higher than the Static-99 estimated risk level of sexual re-offense.

<u>Other Dynamic Empirical Risk Factors</u>

In addition to the static risk factors described above, it is also important to review relevant dynamic risk factors when assessing one's risk for sexual re-offense. A dynamic risk factor refers to something that has the capacity to change over time, for example with treatment. Below is a discussion of dynamic risk factors that are not scored on the Static-99, but have been shown to be significantly related to sexual offense recidivism. These factors are contained in the STABLE-2000, a dynamic risk assessment instrument developed by Hanson and Harris.[5] It should be noted these variables are described below.

5 Hanson, R.K., & Harris, A.J.R. (2001). A structured approach to evaluating change among sexual offenders. *Sexual Abuse, A Journal of Research and Treatment, 13*(2) 105–122.

- Significant Social Influences
- Intimacy Deficits
    - Lovers/Intimate partners
    - Emotional identification with children
    - Social Rejection/Loneliness
    - Lack of concern for others
    - Hostility towards women
- Sexual self-regulation
    - Sex drive/Preoccupation
    - Sex as coping
    - Deviant sexual interests
- Cooperation with supervision
- General self-regulation
    - Impulsive acts
    - Poor cognitive problem-solving skills
    - Negative emotionality/Hostility
- Diagnosed Cluster B Personality Disorder

The nature of an individual's social network is one of the most well-established predictors of criminal behavior. This area is evaluated by examining the **social influences** and support of the individual and assessing whether those people are positive, negative, or neutral influences in regards to supporting pro-social or antisocial behaviors. Negative influences include family, friends, and acquaintances who are criminally involved, gang involved, have substance problems, or who minimize or deny the offender's sex crimes.

In regards to current social contacts, Mr. Miller reported that when he is not in prison he is in contact with his mother, uncles, and friends, and that he is closest to his mother. He reported that he corresponds regularly with his mother, "once in a while" with his uncles, and writes to his sister and brother. He reported that he has "a few" friends, none of whom have a criminal history; however, all of them use amphetamines regularly. His stated plan is to stay away from them upon his release; however, he has been unable to stay away from these friends in the past. He reported that his mother has been sober for 25 years and is his primary support; she sends him money, writes to him, makes purchases for him, and allows him to stay in her home. This factor, then, supports the re-offense risk estimate of the Static-99.

Intimacy deficits are evaluated by examining five components that represent potential problem areas for sexual offenders including lovers/intimate partners, emotional identification with children, social rejection/loneliness, hostility towards women, and lack of concern for others. First, Mr. Miller does not appear to show emotional identification with children, and reports that he has supportive relationships. However, he has previously expressed hostility towards women to the extent that he fantasizes about cutting up and torturing them. Furthermore, he seemed to display a less than average level of concern for others and has never been involved in an intimate relationship. This factor, then, supports the assertion his risk is higher than the Static-99 estimated risk level of sexual re-offense.

Individuals who have poorly controlled sexual impulses are at greater risk for sexual re-offenses. The STABLE-2000 divides sexual self-regulation into three components including sex drive/preoccupation, sex as coping, and deviant sexual interests. Sexual preoccupation focuses on the recurrent sexual thoughts and behaviors that are not directed to a current romantic partner. Relative to these three elements, it is noted that Mr. Miller denied deviant sexual fantasies, a history of sexual preoccupation, and frequent masturbation. However, he has a diagnosis that indicates deviant sexual interest. Taking this into consideration, this cluster supports the assertion that his risk is higher than the Static-99 estimated risk level of sexual re-offense.

An offender's **lack of cooperation with supervision** is related to an increased risk for sexual re-offense. On the STABLE-2000 this was studied for individuals who have been released in the community; however, it is also helpful to examine institutional behavior in regard to cooperation with supervision. Mr. Miller has several known parole violations, including new criminal charges, and has multiple known CDC 115 rules violations. In short, this cluster supports the assertion his risk is higher than the Static-99 estimated risk level of sexual re-offense.

The final component of the STABLE-2000 is composed of **general self-regulation** that is assessed by examining the inmate's impulsivity, problem solving skills, and negative emotionality and hostility. With regards to Mr. Miller, while he does not admit to issues with impulsivity or hostility, his lengthy criminal and violent history indicates that both hostility and lack of problem-solving skills are issues for him. In short, this variable appears to support the assertion his risk is higher than the Static-99 estimated risk level of sexual re-offense.

The diagnostic presence of **Cluster B Personality Disorders** include antisocial, borderline, histrionic, and narcissistic personality disorders, and are associated with increased risk for sexual re-offense. In the case of Mr. Miller, he meets the criteria for Antisocial Personality Disorder, a Cluster B personality disorder. This variable, therefore, appears to support the assertion his risk is higher than the Static-99 estimated level of sexual re-offense.

Protective Factors

There are, additionally, three factors that are considered **protective**. That is, they decrease the risk of further sexual offending. They are: (1) having been in the community without sexually re-offending for a significant period of time; (2) having less than 15 years left in the offender's time at risk due to illness or physical conditions that significantly decrease the motivation and/or ability to sexually re-offend; and (3) having successfully completed a cognitive-behavioral treatment program for sexual offenders.

(1) Having been in the community sex offense free for a significant period of time since committing index sex offense.

Mr. Miller' index offense was committed in 1998; he has not been in the community for a significant period of time since that conviction. Therefore, this potentially protective factor does not apply.

(2) Less than 15 years left in the offender's time at risk due to age or poor health.

Mr. Miller is 35 years old, and is reportedly in good health. This variable, then, is not applicable.

(3) Successful completion of a cognitive-behavioral sexual offender specific treatment program.

Mr. Miller reported that he did not complete a comprehensive cognitive-behavioral sexual offender specific program. This variable, therefore, is not applicable.

Predatory

In addition to formulating an opinion of whether or not Mr. Miller is "likely" to sexually re-offend, it is also important to consider whether or not a sexual re-offense would be "predatory" per the definition of WIC 6600. Specifically, predatory is defined in WIC 6600 as "an act directed toward a stranger, a person of casual acquaintance with whom no substantial relationship exists, or an individual with whom a relationship has been established or promoted for the primary purpose of victimization."

Mr. Miller was convicted for attempting to rape a woman who was a stranger and arrested for attempting to rape two other women who were strangers. Per the Welfare and Institution code the offenses would be considered predatory; therefore, the nature of these relationships is sufficient to support the opinion that, if he does re-offend, it is likely the offense will be predatory.

Alternative Sex Offender Treatment Plans

The California Supreme Court has directed that the following factors should be considered with regards to whether they can be effectively and safely treated in the community: (I) The availability, effectiveness, safety, and practicality of community treatment for the particular disorder the person harbors; (2) Does the person have sufficient volitional power to pursue community treatment voluntarily; (3) Is it reasonable to expect the person to voluntarily pursue community treatment in view of the intended and collateral effects such treatment might entail; (4) Has the person demonstrated treatability and progress in any previous mandatory sex offender-specific treatment; (5) Has the person expressed an intent to seek out and submit to any necessary community treatment.

If released Mr. Miller reported he will have 6 months on parole. When asked how he will stay away from the drug use and criminal behavior, he stated, "Working . . . I think full-time but that might be hard." When asked about his stated plan, he replied, "Be close to my P.O. so I can be easily monitored by him . . . I want to do the right thing." He added that he would not involve himself with people connected to drugs and "join NA."

His long-term plan is to "Raise a family, have kids, be working. I never took life seriously before. This is my only chance." He cited as evidence of his commitment to stay clean from drugs that he stayed at a friend's house where everyone was using methamphetamines when he had been clean for two months and was able to refuse the drugs for 5 days before relapsing. When asked about plans for treatment, he stated that he would be required to attend groups because he was paroling from the EOP program, and that he was "glad about it." He ended by stating, "I don't want to go through this no more. I have another chance. It took 35 years to realize what's going on. I hurt people."

1. There are treatment programs available in the community. There may be a limited number of spaces in California Department of Corrections and Rehabilitation funded High Risk Sex Offender Treatment Programs available to parolees if referred by their parole agent. Additionally, most parole offices offer less intensive forms of sex offender treatment within POC. Effective treatment may or may not be available to him upon his release.

2. Mr. Miller has thus far not sought treatment voluntarily for either his sexual offending or his drug use, in spite of repeated sanctions. He has thus far not demonstrated sufficient volitional power to pursue community treatment voluntarily.

3. Mr. Miller has minimal insight into the factors that would make him a risk to sexually re-offend and he does not believe that he would sexually offend in the future, minimizing the seriousness of his offenses and denying past statements of fantasy. It is unreasonable to expect Mr. Miller to voluntarily participate in sex offender treatment.

4. Mr. Miller has demonstrated minimal progress or insight regarding his sexual problems. He cannot identify the factors (events, thoughts, emotions) that might make him a risk, and he has no reasonable coping strategy to manage his sexual problem. He does not believe that he will re-offend, but

provides no strategy for reducing his risk. Consequently, he has not demonstrated treatability from his previous treatment.

5. It is unclear if, upon his release, Mr. Miller will be compelled to participate in sex offender treatment. He did not express any intention to attend any community-based sex offender treatment programs on his own.

His post-release plan, then, is unlikely to lower his risk of re-offense in the community.

Conclusion Regarding Criterion C

In summary, Mr. Miller scored in the moderate-high range of risk of sexual re-offense on the Static-99R and in the high range of risk of sexual re-offense on the MnSOST-R. These instruments predict whether an offender will be charged with a new sexual offense. Consequently, all of these actuarial instruments underestimate the probability that an offender will commit a new sexual offense. In other words, it is well known that most sexual offenses go unreported and undetected. Therefore, the probability that an offender will commit a new sexual offense is necessarily higher than the probability that he will be detected, arrested, prosecuted, and convicted of committing a new sexual offense.

In consideration of the range of risk on the actuarial instruments, I opine that Mr. Miller is at high risk for sexual re-offense. Additionally, his history is sufficient to support the opinion that, if he does re-offend, it is likely the offense will be predatory. Therefore, in my opinion, Mr. Miller does meet the "likely" standard specified within WIC 6600

Summary

On the Static-99, which reveals the probability that a sex offender will be convicted of a new sexual offense, Mr. Miller scored in the moderate to high range of risk of sexual re-offense. As noted previously, the Static-99 estimate of risk only helps to establish a baseline level of risk and does not take into consideration the many other static and dynamic risk factors explained above. It should also be noted that there is no formal system of adding these variables to the Static-99 risk estimate because of an unknown amount of intercorrelation among the variables. Therefore, in order to determine an individual's risk for sexual recidivism, it is best to begin with the Static-99 estimate and then adjust up or down, depending on the relative presence, absence, and severity of these other variables.

In the case of Mr. Miller, an overall review of these variables support the assertion his risk is higher than the Static-99 estimated risk level of sexual re-offense. Mr. Miller scored in the high range of sexual re-offense on the MnSOST-R, which places him in the high range for offenders who are arrested for a sexual offense in the next six years. This score also supports the assertion his risk is higher than the Static-99 estimated risk level of sexual re-offense. Finally, Mr. Miller is positive for most of the static and dynamic variables; the fact that there were inconsistencies between his self-report and his documented history casts doubt on his report of variables that might have been considered in his favor.

Mr. Miller has been sanctioned for attempting to rape several women over a course of years. His most recent offense involved the use of methamphetamine which he admits raises his level of risk of criminal behavior, impulsivity, and the level of psychosis and which he has had a great deal of difficulty refraining from using. Mr. Miller has a diagnosis of paraphilia NOS, with coercive and sadistic features and has admitted to having fantasies of raping and torturing women, which affects his emotional and volitional capacity such that it predisposes him to the commission of criminal sexual acts in a degree constituting him a menace to the health and safety of others. Finally, the actuarial measures in conjunction with other risk-correlated variables, all together place him at a high risk for sexual re-offense. This is further evidenced by the presence of most of the additional static risk factors, which tend to be robust in predicting long-term risk potential.

For these reasons, Mr. Miller does pose a serious and well-founded risk for sexual re-offense at this time. Additionally, it is my opinion that future sexual offenses are likely to be predatory and Mr. Miller does not appear capable of implementing a personal treatment plan in the community that is sufficient to reduce his risk below the likely standard.

Taking all these variables into consideration, it is my opinion that, if released to the community, Mr. Miller's risk for sexual re-offense falls within the "likely" standard specified within WIC 6600. In short, without appropriate treatment and custody, Mr. Miller is likely to commit another sexually violent and predatory offense.

CONCLUSION

Based on the above information, it is my opinion that Mr. Miller **does meet** the criteria as a sexually violent predator as described in Section 6600(a) of the Welfare and Institutions Code.

Respectfully,
Samantha Stein, Psy.D.
Clinical & Forensic Psychologist
License No. PSY 19074

WELFARE AND INSTITUTIONS CODE SECTION 6600
SEXUALLY VIOLENT PREDATOR CIVIL COMMITMENT

CLINICAL EVALUATION

ADDENDUM
(to the evaluation dated [date])

I. IDENTIFYING INFORMATION:

Name: Luke Miller
Date of Birth: [date, 1974]
CDC Number: [number]
CII Number: [number]
Facility: [County Jail]
EPRD: [date]
CDD: unknown
County of Commitment: [California County]
Interview Date: [date, 2009]
Date Addendum Typed: [date plus 5 months]
DMH Evaluator: Samantha Stein, Psy.D.

This is an Addendum to a commitment evaluation dated [date]. Specifically, documents from Mr. Miller's psychiatric, hospital, forensic and legal records became available and these documents were reviewed to determine whether or not the additional information would alter the findings of the initial evaluation. This examiner was not asked to re-interview Mr. Miller for this addendum.

SOURCES OF INFORMATION:

In addition to the sources of information listed in the prior report, the following documents were reviewed for this addendum report:

[list of 42 titled and dated documents including: DMH Admission/Discharge, Treatment Plans, Assessment, Evaluation, and Treatment reports, Examinations, Memos, Group Therapy Documentation and Reports, Placement Reports, etc.]

II. FINDINGS

Mr. Miller is a 35-year-old man who was convicted for attempting to rape two women and received a parole violation for possibly attempting to assault a third. He was documented as having admitted to regular fantasies of raping women. The initial evaluation by this examiner resulted in the opinion that Mr. Miller suffers from a legally defined mental disorder that predisposes him to committing sexually violent acts. Additionally, the risk estimate of the Static-99, an actuarial risk scale (c.f., prior report), placed Mr. Miller in the medium-high risk category for re-offense. This means he belonged to a group of offenders in the Static-99, 33% of whom were reconvicted for a new sexual offense after five years. The addition of additional variables and other actuarial measures supported the assertion that Mr. Miller's risk of re-offense was higher than the Static-99 estimate of risk. It was the opinion of this examiner that, if released into the community, Mr. Miller is likely to sexually re-offend. With this context in mind, the impact of the additional records will be addressed.

Overall, the available files seemed to support the information that had already been available. The records contained gross discrepancies regarding his diagnoses and history, and his diagnoses changed throughout the records as well. That said, there were important facts that remained consistent throughout the records; these facts, in conjunction with new information available, supports the decisions made previously.

Generally, records seem to be in agreement that Mr. Miller has had "ongoing, deviant sexual fantasies of mutilating and raping women. These fantasies are ongoing, chronic, and pervasive to the patient's record." (DMH Recommended Continuing Care Plan/Discharge Summary, [date]). These "ongoing, chronic, and pervasive fantasies" reported by Mr. Miller, in conjunction with his convictions for attempted rapes, resulted in a diagnosis (also throughout his records) of Paraphilia, NOS, although at times the diagnosis was recorded as provisional. This diagnosis was consistent until the Addendum to Discharge Summary (DMH, [date]), which states that all of his previous diagnoses, including Intermittent Explosive Disorder, Paraphilia, NOS, and all of the various psychotic disorders, can be "better explained" by "the symptoms of a severe personality disorder inclusive of antisocial, borderline, and narcissistic character traits." It states further that "the sexual abuse problem has a sadistic component, but again is better described by his personality disorder." It also concludes that "the affective instability associated with his personality disorder has been managed" with medication.

Of significant note regarding the paraphilic diagnosis is the result of Mr. Miller's psychophysiological testing, or phallometric assessment (PPG) on [date]. The conclusions of this testing state that:

> based on the results of Mr. Miller's phallometric assessment, the presence of a deviant sexual arousal pattern with a preference for aggressive sexual acts directed against an adult female and interest for pubescent females is suggested . . . it is recommended that Mr. Miller be evaluated for anti-androgen treatment and/or behavioral counterconditioning to reduce his deviant sexual arousal responses for aggressive sexual acts directed against an adult female.

Further, in a Psychological Evaluation, dated [date], Mr. Miller is noted to have acknowledged "over 40 sexual liaisons, most of which involved getting a woman so drunk that she was not able to protest his having sex with him." The evaluation concludes that the "level of psychopathology is not severe, but is at the upper limits of the moderate range" and that "current clinical and test data does suggest the presence of an antisocial personality disorder." ([name], Ph.D.)

In regards to a psychotic disorder, a DMH 90-Day Treatment Plan ([date]) revised his diagnosis to exclude such a disorder. The evaluation states that:

> Mr. Miller apparently does not suffer from psychotic symptomatology and has endorsed that he feigned the psychotic symptoms listed in the notes from Department of Corrections (CDC) in order to receive preferential housing and/or to be safe from other prisoners should they find out that he is a sex offender. We have observed Mr. Miller carefully both on and off neuroleptic medications and have found no evidence for truly psychotic symptomatology. We have, however, found the inability to control his temper in several discrete episodes in which he failed to resist aggressive impulses that resulted in assaultive and/or threatening acts. Additionally, the degree of aggressiveness expressed during the episodes was grossly out of proportion to the precipitating psychosocial stressors.

In regards to Mr. Miller's participation in treatment, there is no indication in the available records that he completed sexual offender-specific treatment. Records indicate that he participated in the Sex Offender Treatment Program; however, he dropped out of treatment, requested re-entry, and then did not appear to complete it. The report further states that Mr. Miller

> is uncomfortable with being confronted over cognitive distortions and attitudes regarding interpersonal and sex offending behavior. He dislikes having to accept the label of sex offender and the appellation of rapist.

All of the Mentally Disordered Offender (MDO) evaluations ([date]) were made available, and the conclusion was that he met the criteria and that he "cannot be safely and effectively treated for his severe mental illness on an outpatient basis at this time" because he did "not have adequate control over his impulses." The DMH Addendum to Discharge Summary ([date]) notes that he no longer met the criteria for hospitalization under the MDO criteria (due to the change in his diagnosis); however, it was recommended that "he have a highly supervised parole, given his history of violence and harm to others." This was prior to his parole violation for attempting to force entry into a woman's home.

There remain various other inconsistencies within the records. For example, a DMH Neurological Report ([date]) states that Mr. Miller had "some major limitations" in regards to neurological functioning and intelligence, and "it is likely that he had either fetal alcohol exposure or perhaps lead exposure as a child." Additionally, there was reportedly a "prevalence of mental illness" in his family, including his brother, mother, and father, who "allegedly . . . has required extensive psychiatric hospitalizations." This history or neurological symptomatology is not noted in other records; the results of the EEG are not known. This is only one of many instances where information about Mr. Miller's reported psychosocial history, level of functioning, and/or symptomatology vary dramatically from other reports. In the interview with this examiner, for example, Mr. Miller reported no history of mental illness in his family. Additionally, he was able to complete tasks that he had been previously reported to be unable to.

DIAGNOSED MENTAL DISORDER (Revised)

The results of this addendum indicate Mr. Miller has the following revised diagnostic profile:

Axis I	302.9	Paraphilia Not Otherwise Specified (NOS), with Coercive and Sadistic Features
	304.40	Amphetamine Dependence, With Physiological Dependence
	305.00	Alcohol Abuse
Axis II	301.7	Antisocial Personality Disorder

Overall, the information provided in the additional records did not contradict the findings of the prior report, and does not change Mr. Miller's score on the actuarial risk scale. What remains is a well-documented history of a man who has reported pervasive fantasies of raping and torturing women in combination with two and possibly three attempts to rape a woman, whose scores on the available actuarial measures and variables indicate he is at high risk for sexual re-offense. After reviewing the issues described above, it remains this examiner's opinion that Mr. Miller continues to meet the criteria for civil commitment pursuant to WIC 6600. For a much more detailed description of Mr. Miller's case, please refer to the prior report by this examiner.

CONCLUSION

Based on the above information, it is my opinion that Mr. Miller **does meet** the criteria as a sexually violent predator as described in Section 6600(a) of the Welfare and Institutions Code.

Respectfully Submitted,
Samantha Stein, Psy.D.
Clinical & Forensic Psychologist
License No. PSY 1907

NOTICE OF EVALUATION
AS A SEXUALLY VIOLENT PREDATOR

You are being evaluated to determine whether you may be a Sexually Violent Predator (SVP) under Section 6600 of the California Welfare and Institutions Code. The purpose of the evaluation and interview is to decide if you have a mental condition that makes you likely to commit sexual crimes in the future. If you are determined to meet the criteria for the SVP law, you could be sent to court for trial. If the court finds you to be an SVP, you would not be released from custody. You would be sent to a treatment program at a state mental hospital for two years. This would be an involuntary commitment to a sex offender treatment program run by the California Department of Mental Health. The commitment can be renewed every two years. If you are currently committed as an SVP, this evaluation may be for the purpose of determining whether you continue to meet the criteria for commitment. The commitment would end and you would be released from the treatment program when the court determines you are no longer likely to commit sexual crimes.

You will be evaluated by two doctors (psychologists or psychiatrists). Their job is to provide an unbiased assessment of your risk to commit future sexual crimes. Both doctors must decide that you meet legal criteria as an SVP for the Department of Mental Health to recommend your commitment to the District Attorney in the county which last sentenced you to prison. If the District Attorney decides not to file the case, you will be paroled, or released from custody. If the District Attorney decides to file a petition for commitment, your case will go to court. A defense attorney would then be appointed to defend you and protect your rights under the law. Based on the outcome of the court proceedings, you may be paroled or committed to the treatment program.

If the two doctors disagree whether you qualify as an SVP, one or two additional doctors will evaluate you. The doctors conduct their evaluations independently, and do not consult with each other while preparing their evaluations.

The evaluation includes review of your records, an interview, and sometimes psychological testing. The interview is voluntary. The doctors will write reports on your case, and may later testify if your case goes to court. Any information you provide during an interview may be used in the doctor's reports and court testimony. If you give any new information about abuse of children or elders that has not been previously reported, the doctors are legally required to report this information to the authorities. If you do not consent to the interview, the evaluation will be completed using only your records.

I have been informed about my evaluation as a Sexually Violent Predator and I have been offered a copy of this notification.

(check) _____

I (circle) **agree / do not agree** to be interviewed by Dr._____

_____   _____

Date   Inmate's Signature

_____   _____

Date   Evaluator's Signature

Evaluator: Describe any reasonable accommodation provided to the person being evaluated.

Acknowledgments

I FOUND MYSELF JOURNALING. I was doing work that was incredibly challenging and complex, ethically fraught, fascinating, and had wide-reaching implications. And so, in the in-between places (airports, hotel rooms, prison lobbies) I found myself writing about it. To make sense of it. And because I craved a deeper conversation about it. Thus, the beginnings of this book were formed.

It's been years and drafts between that journaling and now, and I'm deeply grateful for the help I've had getting here. I've tried to include everyone here but of course there are many who, undoubtedly, are left out. Please know it's not for lack of appreciation in my heart.

I've always had the desire to write and make art as much, if not more, as I've wanted to be a psychologist. Thus, it's a dream-come-true for me to have one passion launch me into the other. I have the memoirists who've come before me to thank for this. So many of you have inspired me and shown me it's possible to write about something important while touching people. And how to write it well. Thank you.

To that end, I also want to express deep gratitude to my agent, Leslie Meredith, at Dystel, Goderich & Bourret. You had complete confidence in me from day one, and have held me, and this book, with the greatest of care, every step of the way on its journey into the hands of readers. Thank you from the bottom of my heart.

Similarly, I owe deep thanks to Denise Silvestro and the team at Kensington Books: Robert Yaffe's design, production editor Robin Cook, publicist extraordinaire Ann Pryor, publisher Jackie Dinas, and head honcho Steve Zacharius. Denise, you understood immediately what I wanted to say with this book and believed in it. Then, with your guidance, we made it into something even better–a book that would reach the most people possible—without ever making me feel like I was compromising what was most important. A feat worthy of a gold star if I ever gave them out. Not only that, you allowed my art to be a part of what I had to offer. Thank you.

While I don't have an MFA, that doesn't mean I haven't worked on my craft, and I have many to thank for their guidance and encouragement in this regard. The Community of Writers read part of an early draft of this book and accepted me into their prestigious program, accompanying me on my journey to feeling like a Real Writer. I'm grateful to Anxy Magazine and the Guardian, who published early excerpts, building my confidence that there was a waiting audience for this book. Mark Weinstein, Stephen Power, and the excellent team at Kevin Anderson & Associates believed in this project and assisted me in shaping it into a saleable package. Nomi Isak, Josh Mohr, Dinah Berland, Jonathan Santlofer, Arielle Estuck, The Writer's Grotto, Writing Salon, Tara Reale, Rebecca Brown, HS, and so many others believed in my writing and my message, made me a better writer, and made this a better book.

In my career as a psychologist, I've been truly blessed to be mentored and surrounded by brilliant minds who do their work with impeccable ethics, all while holding the nuance and the gray even when it's hard. Thank you to Drs. Mary-Perry Miller and Tom Tobin who saw the potential in me to do this work even before I saw it in myself. The late Charles Flinton, PhD, was my mentor and friend, and taught me so much more than I ever could've learned in school—through both his teaching and his role modeling. Chuck, Mark Koetting, PhD, Elizabeth Corsale, MFT, Michael Nold, MFT, Jennifer Fernandez, PhD, Dan Doyle, MFT, Dale Arnold, PhD and fellow SVP panel members, my colleagues at Sharper Future and Pathways Institute, and all of my other compatriots in forensic psychology, thank you for all you've taught me about what it means to do this work with integrity while maintaining our compassion and humanity. I also have gratitude for those in all parts of the criminal justice system—those police officers, probation and parole, correctional officers, attorneys, judges–who work to keep society safer without losing their compassion.

Over the many years I've been in practice I've had hundreds of people trust me with their stories, their deepest secrets, and their inner worlds. Thank you for entrusting me with your hearts, for allowing me to walk with you through your struggles, and for inspiring me to be my best self. This book would not exist without you.

I am grateful, every day (twice a day) for Maharishi Mahesh Yogi's gift of Transcendental Meditation. My life, and my ability to live fully and witness it–to break out of my own internal prisons–is because I have this practice. D, you held down the fort and supported me doing this crazy work while I lived this story and wrote it. Thank you. Cannon Thomas, PhD, of CTP Strategies, from day one you knew I would get here and you steadfastly helped me in the best way possible: through guiding me into a discovery of my most authentic self. I could not be more grateful.

Finally, and in the most basic sense, I could not have written this book without those in my life who loved, supported, and believed in me, even when my choice of profession baffled or frightened them. Who helped me wrestle with good and evil and right and wrong, and held me in the in-between. Who supported me as I continued to believe this book was worthy of being brought into the world, even as I wasn't sure the rest of the world thought that.

Without my friends who are family and my family who are friends, I would never have the courage and fortitude to write a book, let alone bring it into the world. Catherine, you've walked beside me since we weren't yet fully formed, inspiring, encouraging, and loving me unconditionally all along the way, every day. I'm here because of us. Elizabeth, you are always there with love, through thick and thin, always helping me remember who's the Real Boss. Melanie, Marcia, Michelle, Dan, Ariella, Dean, Steven, Marco, Stef, Lisa, the Institute of Vedic Psychology crew, my recovery fellowship, you've been inspiring, loving, supportive, and indispensable companions on my journey. My beloved John, your unwavering belief in me and profound support, as you lovingly walk by my side, brings such joy and comfort to my heart. Also, it's important even for forensic psychologists to have fun sometimes; I'm so grateful you invite me, with humor, on adventure every day.

My parents have never doubted I could do what I set my mind to, and have given me nothing but their full love and support at every turn–even when walking into prisons to meet with violent sex offenders made them a little nervous. Mom and Dad, I'm deeply fortunate to have you as my parents. Dearest Matthew, it's because you've been with me our whole lives that I am here and I am me. You inspire, teach, support, and love me in all ways and remind me how incredible it is to be human. I thank my lucky stars I've always had you.

Finally, I have deep gratitude for my awesome kids: you've always inspired me to be my best self and to keep making the world a better place. Your openness continually helps your mom do this intense work without losing faith in humanity. Because of you, I continue to see the beauty even in all the ugly–you've always been beacons of light even on the darkest of days.